I0880370

THE BRITANNICA GUIDE TO THE SOCIAL SCIENCES

ECONOMICS

EDITED BY

SHAUN SETH

Britannica Educational Publishing

IN ASSOCIATION WITH

ROSEN

EDUCATIONAL SERVICES

Published in 2016 by Britannica Educational Publishing (a trademark of Encyclopædia Britannica, Inc.) in association with The Rosen Publishing Group, Inc.
29 East 21st Street, New York, NY 10010

Distributed exclusively by Rosen Publishing.
To see additional Britannica Educational Publishing titles, go to rosenpublishing.com.

First Edition

Britannica Educational Publishing
J.E. Luebering: Director, Core Reference Group
Anthony L. Green: Editor, Compton's by Britannica

Rosen Publishing
Shaun Seth: Editor
Nelson Sá: Art Director
Brian Garvey: Designer
Cindy Reiman: Photography Manager
Karen Huang: Photo Researcher

Library of Congress Cataloging-in-Publication Data

Economics / edited by Shaun Seth.
pages cm. — (The Britannica guide to the social sciences)
Includes bibliographical references and index.
ISBN 978-1-62275-542-4 (library bound)
1. Economics--Juvenile literature. I. Seth, Shaun. II. Title.
HB183.E263 2016
330--dc23

2015017711

Manufactured in the United States of America

Photo credits: Cover, p. 1 marigold_88/iStock/Thinkstock; pp. vii, 21, 22, 23, 37, 52, 63, 73 Encyclopaedia Britannica, Inc.; p. 2 The Asahi Shimbun/Getty Images; p. 12 Bloomberg/Getty Images; pp. 29, 34, 127 © Photos.com/Thinkstock; p. 32 Courtesy of The National Portrait Gallery, London; p. 43 Tim Gidal/Picture Post/Getty Images; p. 58 PhotoStock-Israel/Photolibrary/Getty Images; pp. 60, 132 © AP Images; p. 65 Joe Raedle/Getty Images; p. 68 George Rose/Hulton Archive/Getty Images; p. 76 Andrew Burton/Getty Images; p. 84 Spencer Platt/Getty Images; p. 89 Konstantin Sutyagin/Shutterstock.com; p. 95 Nigel Pavitt/AWL Images/Getty Images; p. 100 Private Collection/© Look and Learn/Bridgeman Images; p. 102 © The British Library/The Image Works; p. 109 Mary Evans/Science Source; p. 114 Don Emmert/AFP/Getty Imags; p. 117 Culture Club/Hulton Archive/Getty Images; p. 124 Brendan Smialowski/AFP/Getty Images; p. 134 Jianan Yu/Reuters/Landov

CONTENTS

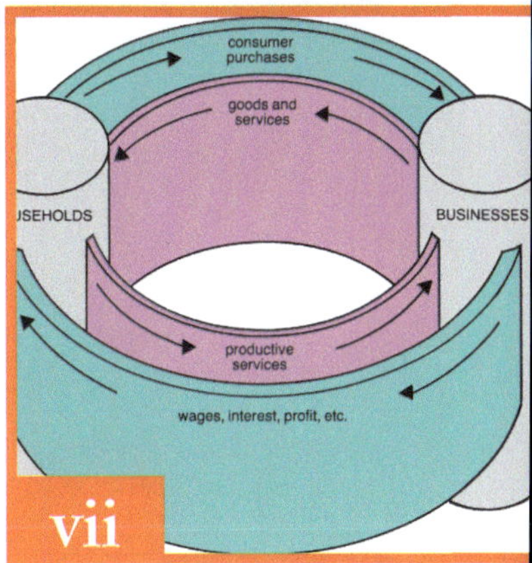

vii

12

32

60

68

89

95

124

134

INTRODUCTION

As a social science that studies how a society's resources are shared, economics (a) describes and analyzes choices about the way goods and services are produced, distributed, and consumed, and (b) assesses the consequences of those choices. The word "economics" comes from the Greek *oikos*, meaning "household," and *nomos*, meaning "rule," or "governance." Thus "household management"—the performance of the tasks and services that allow a family to survive and prosper—refers to those economic activities devoted to satisfying the primary needs of food, clothing, and shelter. Such needs are common to all human beings.

Economic functions also satisfy desires for goods and services that are not essential needs but that people choose to buy. Such goods and services are often called luxuries, but most goods are more accurately considered neither luxuries nor necessities. Additionally goods, such as automobiles, mobile phones, and visits to the dentist, that might be seen as luxuries in one country may be considered necessities in another.

By studying the means through which goods and services are provided, economists come to understand more about entire economies. There have been economies since the dawn of civilization, but economics is a recently developed field of study. It originated as a discipline during the 18th century when Scottish moral philosopher Adam Smith published his classic study *An Inquiry into the Nature and Causes of the Wealth of Nations* (1776).

An economy is the wealth-producing segment of society. Wealth is defined as the total sum of all possessions (including financial assets) minus total liabilities. Where it is possible to attach a value to every possession, wealth can be measured in terms of money. Although money is best understood as a means of exchange, it may be called the economic equivalent of wealth. Economies exist because human beings have needs and desires. These are satisfied by the production of goods—all of which express a society's wealth.

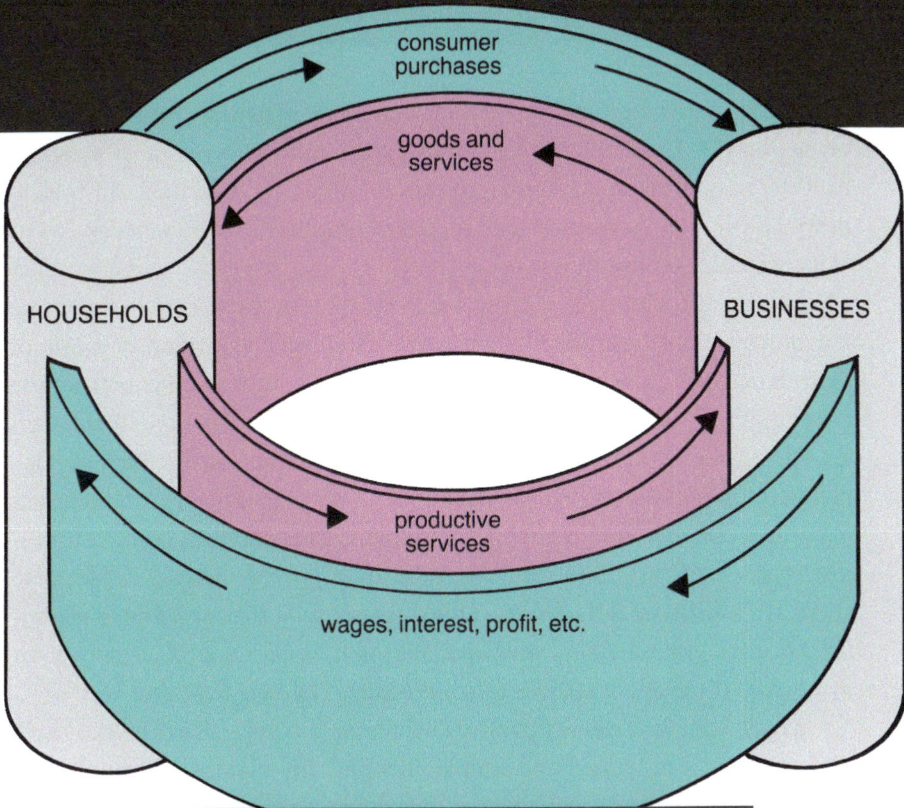

Diagram illustrating the flow of money, goods, and services in a modern industrial economy.

From the earliest days of civilization, all societies have had economic arrangements to satisfy the needs and desires of their populations. In fact, the economic problem of production and distribution can be summarized by four questions that all economic systems must answer: What goods and services will be produced? How will they be produced? For whom will they be produced? How will they be distributed?

Contemporary economists identify three distinct economic systems—tradition-based, command, and market. In economies governed by tradition, as in monarchies, personal advancement is unlikely and social roles are rigid.

Command systems, on the other hand, mobilize resources and labour in ways far beyond the reach of traditional societies, so that societies with command systems typically boast of large-scale achievements such as the Great Wall of China or the Egyptian pyramids. The amount of personal freedom in command economies, however, often can be limited. Socialism, in which the state owns the major modes of production, represents one form of a command economy.

In the third mode—the market economy, or capitalism—economic outcomes are not controlled by any one person (such as a ruler) or group of persons (such as a central planning committee) but instead emerge from the "workings" of the system itself. In fact, they actually come about through the efforts of individuals seeking personal gain and financial reward by supplying the things that others are willing to pay for. Historically, after decades of competition between planned and unplanned economies (as in communist versus capitalist countries), the latter have proved themselves far more adept at creating wealth. A reason for this success is that unplanned economies depend on individual initiative, personal ambition, and ingenuity. In most cases these opportunities exist because of political freedom.

Many contemporary economies represent a combination of the three basic economic systems. For example, in a partially planned economy such as China's, the government frequently encourages specific types of companies, such as manufacturers, and gives assistance to these firms in the form of tax-funded subsidies that help them develop new product lines, build new plants, or expand their operations. Governments also can promote investment and regulate trade so as to favour domestic manufacturers. Socialism at the turn of the 21st century proved less attractive than democratic capitalism, but many socialist concepts were nonetheless incorporated into free-market systems, as evidenced by public support for spending on social programs.

The earliest economic systems operated under a traditional system. Such societies themselves were political, religious, and military units made up of the rulers and the ruled. It was the ruled—labourers, slaves, peasants, or craftsmen—who produced the wealth, and most of their wealth went toward the enrichment of the ruling classes.

Late in the Middle Ages a number of factors slowly came together to create the modern economic system called capitalism. Among these factors were the emergence of international banking, the creation of overseas colonial empires, expanded international trade, the growing independence of peasants from the landed aristocracy, and the gradually lessened control of governments over economic functions. To these was added in the 18th century the start of the Industrial Revolution. This was the most potent agent of economic change. It transformed societies completely, eventually challenging the power of monarchies and bringing about the concept of the middle class.

Convenient and random economic arrangements were changed into an economic system. Nearly everything in society became a commodity to be bought or sold. As people became free to specialize in certain types of work or seek jobs with different employers, labour itself was uprooted from its fixed place on land or in guilds. In effect, labour became a commodity. People offered their services to employers, who paid them instead of extracting wealth from them by force. Individuals or families worked for business owners, not rulers. Societies had become economies.

There were still political, military, and other institutional arrangements, but the broadest well-being of a society could now be measured by its economic function. Societies were rapidly expanding marketplaces that existed primarily for the creation of wealth. People could see themselves as having a stake in society—a chance to raise their status and to obtain some wealth for themselves.

The United States is an example of an unplanned economy. This does not mean, however, that there is no government involvement in economic functions. As the economy of the United States grew, and as government and its scope of responsibility increased, it was inevitable that government policy at every level would affect economic functions through regulations intended to achieve such goals as job safety and air pollution control.

Nevertheless, the economy of the United States can be considered unplanned because the government does not mandate what will be produced or how it will be marketed. These decisions are left largely to the private sector. Even the enormous amount of government regulation that has emerged since the Great Depression of the 1930s has not turned the United States into a planned economy.

Capitalism is the only economic system in the world that can operate within a variety of political systems. It can be called a system because it embraces all of society and because it operates on its own terms. Although capitalism is commonly associated with democracy, it does not depend upon government or any other traditional institutional framework for its continuation.

The debate between planned and unplanned economies, however, is uneven. It is really a clash between an assortment of political systems and one economic system.

The chief economic problem of a planned economy (such as in socialism) centres on the inability to foresee all future needs. Because of this, a planned economy fails in the efficient performance of the task for which its planning apparatus exists—namely, the effective coordination of production and distribution. However attractive a planned economy might be in theory, in practice it is impossible, because it would depend on a huge planning agency capable of making the millions of coordinated decisions necessary to produce the gigantic catalog of goods and services demanded in modern society. Furthermore, in planned economies lacking private property rights, there are few incentives to succeed. This was evident in the Soviet Union in the late 1980s, when growing numbers of people lacked the motivation to put all of their labour toward efforts that would not reward them.

Capitalism is not without its critics, some of whom have alleged that the capitalist system suffers from inherent instability: Because capitalist growth is driven by profit expectations, it experiences unpredictable highs and lows as economic booms meet their inevitable end. In the "bust" that follows, people lose jobs, opportunities are lost, and investments lose their value until the growth phase of the next business cycle begins.

A second criticism focuses on the adverse side effects of a profit-driven system. For example, many production processes generate "bads" as well as "goods," such as toxic wastes or unhealthy working conditions. The argument can be made that market growth, because it is focused on profit, is therefore blind to such negative effects.

A third criticism of capitalist growth concerns the fairness with which capitalism distributes its expanding wealth and shares its hardships. People earn different wages for different work, with corporate executives typically earning vastly more income than ordinary office or factory employees. Pointing to a different problem, critics question a system that counts every dollar of input and output but pays no heed to moral, social, or aesthetic qualities of the items being produced.

If an economy is not planned, how can it be managed? No one seems to be in control. There are, in fact, many controls, but the prime control within capitalism is called the marketplace. A market is composed of two factors: supply and demand. Economists have not been able to agree on which one predominates. In reality supply and demand probably alternate. Sometimes a popular demand calls forth a product; at other times a supply creates a demand.

The economies of modern industrial nations are large and complex. To be sure, there is management, and there are market forces at work, but there are also many other factors that help or hinder economic function.

In modern industrial societies governments play a large role. There is a great amount of regulation, most of it meant for the protection of the public. All regulations affect the way businesses operate, often increasing their costs and reducing their profits. Lower profits, in turn, reduce the amount of money—which is known as working capital—that a company can use for expansion.

Auto emission standards, for instance, have had a significant impact on the manufacture and pricing of automobiles, but they have also had a positive impact on human health. Other government policies—such as taxation, budget deficits, and regulation of the money supply—have an effect on how much money is available for people to spend on goods and services.

International crises and other conditions also affect the working of an economy. War can cut off the supply of such resources as petroleum, chromium, or copper. Weather affects agriculture: A hot, dry summer can damage the wheat crop, and floods can destroy thousands of acres of crops suddenly.

People's attitudes also have an impact on the marketing of goods. Health-conscious individuals, for example, may stop smoking, curtail their intake of alcohol, and avoid unhealthy foods. Advertising affects what people buy, and it can create a market where none existed. Style and fashion are significant for many consumers.

There are other economic problems that are more difficult to understand, such as the "boom and bust" alternations of the business cycle. Although periods of prosperity can be explained rather easily, the reasons for panics, recessions, and depressions are complex. So many factors contributed to the Great Depression of the 1930s, for example, that economists often disagree on the cause of that prolonged economic downturn.

Because the causes of decline are uncertain, the remedies are equally uncertain. In the early 21st century all industrialized societies through their governments shared a goal of stabilizing economies, keeping them prosperous, and reducing unemployment. None of the remedies worked to the extent that was hoped. How economies work and what remedies can be found to keep them operating efficiently are the tasks of economists, who must work together with business leaders and politicians.

What follows in the pages ahead is an overview of the fundamentals and development of economics, a survey of the problems addressed by economists today, and an examination of the growth of various economic systems around the world.

CHAPTER ONE

FOUNDATIONS OF ECONOMICS

Economics is a social science that seeks to analyze and describe the production, distribution, and consumption of wealth. In the 19th century, economics was the hobby of gentlemen of leisure and the vocation of a few academics; economists wrote about economic policy but were rarely consulted by legislators before decisions were made. Today there is hardly a government, international agency, or large commercial bank that does not have its own staff of economists. Many of the world's economists devote their time to teaching economics in colleges and universities around the world, but most work in various research or advisory capacities, either for themselves (in economics consulting firms), in industry, or in government. Still others are employed in accounting, commerce, marketing, and business administration; although they are trained as economists, their occupational expertise falls within other fields. Indeed, this can be considered "the age of economists," and the demand for their services seems insatiable. Supply responds to that demand, and in the United States alone some 400 institutions of higher learning grant about 900 new Ph.D.'s in economics each year.

DEFINITION

No one has ever succeeded in neatly defining the scope of economics. Many have agreed with Alfred Marshall, a leading 19th-century English economist, that economics is "a study of mankind in the ordinary business of life; it examines that part of individual and social action which is most closely connected with the attainment, and with the use of the material requisites of wellbeing"—ignoring the fact that sociologists, psychologists, and anthropologists frequently study exactly the same phenomena. In the 20th century, English economist Lionel Robbins defined economics as "the science which studies human behaviour as a relationship between (given) ends and scarce means which have alternative uses." In other words, Robbins said that economics is the science of economizing. While his definition captures one of the striking characteristics of the economist's way of thinking, it is at once too wide (because it would include in economics the game of chess) and too narrow (because it would exclude the study of the national income or the price level). Perhaps the only foolproof definition is that attributed to Canadian-born economist Jacob Viner: Economics is what economists do.

The assembly line, first pioneered by Ford Motors in the 1910s, is still used to produce cars today.

Difficult as it may be to define economics, it is not difficult to indicate the sorts of questions that concern economists. Among other things, they seek to analyze the forces determining prices—not only the prices of goods and services but the prices of the resources used to produce them. This involves the discovery of two key elements: what governs the way in which human labour, machines, and land are combined in production and how buyers and sellers are brought together in a functioning market. Because prices of the various things must be interrelated, economists therefore ask how such a "price system" or "market mechanism" hangs together and what conditions are necessary for its survival.

These questions are representative of microeconomics, the part of economics that deals with the behaviour of individual entities such as consumers, business firms, traders, and farmers. The other major branch of economics is macroeconomics, which focuses attention on aggregates such as the level of income in the whole economy, the volume of total employment, the flow of total investment, and so forth. Here economists are concerned with the forces determining the income of a country or the level of total investment, and they seek to learn why full employment is so rarely attained and what public policies might help a country achieve higher employment or greater price stability.

But these examples still do not exhaust the range of problems that economists consider. There is also the important field of development economics, which examines the attitudes and institutions supporting the process of economic development in poor countries as well as those capable of self-sustained economic growth (for example, development economics was at the heart of the Marshall Plan). In this field the economist is concerned with the extent to which the factors affecting economic development can be manipulated by public policy.

Cutting across these major divisions in economics are the specialized fields of public finance, money and banking, international trade, labour economics, agricultural economics, industrial organization, and others. Economists are frequently consulted to assess the effects of governmental measures such as taxation, minimum-wage laws, rent controls, tariffs, changes in interest rates, changes in government budgets, and so on.

SCARCITY: RESOURCE LIMITATIONS AND ALLOCATION

The modern industrial economy is characterized by a high degree of interdependence of its parts. The supplier of components or raw materials, for example, must deliver the desired quantities of his products at the right moment and in the desired specifications. In economies such as those of western Europe, North America, and Japan, the coordination of these activities is done through the price system. The relative prices of the various inputs (e.g., labour, materials, machinery) tend to determine the proportions in which they will be used. Prices also affect the relative outputs of the various final products, and they determine who will consume them.

The fact that goods have value can be ascribed ultimately to the limitations in the world's material endowment. Human beings do not have all the arable land, petroleum, or platinum that they would like; their use must be rationed. That is why goods have prices; if they were available in unlimited supply they would be free. Price usually serves as the rationing device whereby their use is kept down to the available supply.

Resources can be said to be scarce in both an absolute and in a relative sense: the surface of the Earth is finite, imposing absolute scarcity; but the scarcity that concerns economists is the relative scarcity of resources in different uses. Materials used for one purpose cannot at the same time be used for other purposes; if the quantity of an input is limited, the increased use of it in one manufacturing process must cause it to become scarcer in other uses.

The cost of a product in terms of money may not measure its true cost to society. The true cost of, say, the construction of a supersonic jet is the value of the schools and refrigerators that will never be built as a result. Every act of production uses up some of society's available resources; it means the foregoing of an opportunity to produce something else. In deciding how to use resources most effectively to satisfy the wants of the community, this opportunity cost (that is, the opportunities forgone in the choice of one expenditure over others) must ultimately be taken into account.

In a market economy the relationship between the price of a good and the quantity supplied depends on the cost of making it, and that cost, ultimately, is the cost of *not* making other goods. The market mechanism enforces this relationship. In the first instance, the cost of, say, a pair of shoes is the price of the leather, the labour, the fuel, and other elements used up in producing them. But the price of these inputs, in turn, depends on what they can produce elsewhere—if the handbags that can be produced with the leather are valued very highly by consumers, the price of leather will be bid up correspondingly.

THE PRICE SYSTEM

A price system is a means of organizing economic activity. It does this primarily by coordinating the decisions of consumers, producers, and owners of productive resources. Millions of economic agents who have no direct communication with each other are led by the price system to supply each other's wants. In a modern economy the price system enables a consumer to buy a product he has never previously purchased, produced by a firm of whose existence he is unaware, which is operating with funds partially obtained from his own savings.

Prices are an expression of the consensus on the values of different things, and every society that permits exchanges between people has prices. Because prices are expressed in terms of a widely acceptable commodity, they permit a ready comparison of the comparative values of various commodities—if shoes are $15 per pair and bread 30 cents per loaf, a pair of shoes is worth 50 loaves of bread. The price of anything is its value in exchange for a commodity of wide acceptability: the price of an automobile may be some 50 ounces of gold or 25 pieces of paper currency.

A system of prices exists because individual prices are related to each other. If, for example, copper rods cost 40 cents a pound and the process of drawing a rod into wire costs 25 cents a pound, then it will be profitable to produce wire from a copper rod if its price exceeds 65 cents. Conversely, it will be unprofitable to produce wire if its price falls below 65 cents. Competition will hold the price of wire about 25 cents per pound above that of rods. A variety of such economic forces tie the entire structure of prices together.

The system of prices can be arranged to reward or penalize any kind of activity. Society discourages the production of electric shoestring-tying machines by the simple expedient of making such a machine's attainable selling price less than the prices of the resources necessary to produce it. Society stimulates people of great athletic promise to learn golf (rather than polo or cricket) by awarding significant prizes (= prices) to tournament winners. The air in many cities is dirty because no one is charged a price for polluting it and no one can pay a price for having it cleaned.

THE BASIC FUNCTIONS OF ECONOMIC SYSTEMS

Every economic system provides solutions to four questions: what goods and services will be produced; how they will be produced; for whom they will be produced; and how they will be allocated between consumption (for present use) and investment (for future use). In a decentralized (usually private enterprise) economic system, these questions are resolved, and economic coordination is achieved, through the price mechanism.

PRODUCT AND QUANTITY

Even the simpler economy of a traditional society must choose between food and shelter, weapons and tools, or priests and hunters. In a modern economy the potential variety of goods and services that may be produced is immense. Consider, for example, the thousands of new book titles that are published each year—or the hundreds of colours of paint or the thousands of styles of clothing that are brought to the market annually. Each of these actual collections is much smaller than the amount that could be produced.

A price system weighs the desires of consumers in terms of the prices they are willing to pay for various quantities of each commodity or service. The payment for the services of a skilled surgeon (a price much influenced by the number of surgeons) reflects the unique nature of those skills for the buyer-patient, whereas the price of an electric popcorn popper reflects the minor convenience it provides. Of course, the amount consumers agree to pay will be influenced by their wealth as well as their desires, but for any single consumer, relative desire is proportional to the price offered.

Universal laws are not common in social life. Economists nonetheless place immense confidence in the proposition that the consumer will buy less of any commodity when its price rises. This law of demand is by no means a necessary fact of life; rather it is an empirical rule to which there are no known, reliable exceptions. Bread, caviar, education, narcotics—interested buyers will purchase more of each when its price falls. These demand prices are the guides that in effect tell producers which items to produce and in what quantities.

PRODUCTION

The second question an economy must answer involves deciding how the desired goods are to be produced. There is more than one way to grow

EFFICIENCY

In economics and organizational analysis, efficiency is a measure of the input a system requires to achieve a specified output. A system that uses few resources to achieve its goals is efficient, in contrast to one that wastes much of its input.

Efficiency is a favourite objective of economists and administrators, but not everyone agrees on its meaning. Claims of inefficiency are submitted regularly in many policy debates, but each participant believes that his or her own proposal is the most efficient. In all cases, the disputants agree that efficiency is desirable. Whatever the goals, they should be achieved with as little input or cost as necessary. When it comes to measuring efficiency or creating an efficient system, however, the consensus quickly evaporates. Judging means to ends is a difficult prospect, and arguments disguised as conflicts over efficiency are often deeper conflicts over appropriate goals, social systems, or views of human nature.

There is a fundamental disciplinary debate about the likelihood of efficiency in organizations, however. Economists generally believe that organizations are efficient; they rationally allocate resources and optimally respond to their environments. Sociologists often believe that organizations are merely effective; they aim for survival and often use suboptimal arrangements that satisfy the social needs of participants and surrounding institutions. This empirical debate about the likelihood of efficiency often creeps into the differing applications of the term.

In economic contexts, measuring efficiency means asking whether the monetary evaluation of the inputs used to produce some goal are the minimal possible costs associated with achieving that goal. If something is called inefficient, it means that the goal could have been reached with less cost or that the goal could have been better achieved (in some monetarily measurable fashion) with the same costs. Economists assume that costs and benefits will be measured in some currency, but the proper weighting of costs and benefits is left to another debate. This notion is more specifically measured via the concept of x-efficiency, which is defined as the degree to which a group of inputs achieves the maximal level of outputs possible with those inputs. Market theory predicts that all firms will be x-efficient under perfect competition, because competitors would drive x-inefficient firms out of business over long periods.

Common theories in social welfare economics use more specific types of efficiency to evaluate allocation systems. A system is called Pareto optimal if no exchange can be made that will make one person better off without making someone else worse off. Unequal allocations are typically still Pareto optimal because those endowed with resources would lose something if their wealth was redistributed. A system is called Kaldor-Hicks efficient if resources are put in the hands of those that value them the most, measured by whether one person could theoretically compensate another for the same resources at a cost that would be worth it to them but worth more than the traded resources to the seller. This criterion is one way to think about allocative efficiency, or maximizing the aggregate value of a resource allocation. Economists will evaluate potential changes based on whether the net benefit of resources increases as the resources are put to use by all individuals.

wheat, train lawyers, refine petroleum, and transport baggage. The efficient production of goods and services requires that certain fundamental rules be followed: no resource should be used in producing one thing when it could be producing something more valuable elsewhere, and each product should be made with the smallest-possible amount of resources.

A functioning price system induces all participants in the economy to steer their resources toward activities that yield a reward. Jobs that pay a high price for labour will attract workers seeking the reward of a high salary. Crops that yield a greater profit will attract more farmers to cultivate them. Similarly, capital will be drawn from a faltering trade and redirected to an industry where it can earn higher returns.

This same price system seeks to achieve production efficiency through competition. If one firm, for instance, can design, produce, and distribute shoes while using fewer resources than its rivals, it will make larger profits; it is therefore motivated to discover more efficient combinations of inputs and plant locations, to devise wage systems to stimulate its workers, to use computers to manage inventories and streamline shipping, and so forth.

DISTRIBUTION

The third question an economy answers involves determining who gets the product. For example, if family A acquires $5,000 worth of goods this year and family B receives five times as much, how is this division to be decided? The incomes of individuals are determined by the quantities of resources (labour skills, capital in all its forms) they own and the prices they receive for the use of these resources. Workers are encouraged by the price system to acquire new skills and to exercise them diligently, and families are encouraged to save (capital accumulation) because of the rewards paid as interest or dividends. Inherited ability and wealth also contribute to the distribution of income.

If the price system is working reasonably well (some of the common failures will be noted later), it performs all of these economic functions with remarkable subtlety and precision. Society desires not only the correct amount of wheat but also that it be consumed more or less evenly over the crop year, with a surplus to carry over in case of a partial failure of the next year's crop. The price system provides a seasonal price pattern that encourages the holding of inventories rather than early splurging and richly rewards speculators who correctly anticipate a crop failure and hold grain that will alleviate it. In the same way, the desires of every sizable group of consumers (or resource owners) are registered through the price system; entrepreneurs are incited by price offers to provide opera and musical comedy, kosher food, and Persian delicacies. One might almost say that the price system is devoted to minority rule, since the only pressure toward uniformity is in the possibility of lowering costs of production by standardizing goods.

High prices in a properly functioning price system thus serve as incentives to produce more and consume less, and lower prices serve as corresponding deterrents. In addition the price system is a method of communicating information. The English philosopher Herbert Spencer once stated, rather ponderously, that only by constant iteration can alien truths be impressed upon reluctant minds: The price system, with its capacity for infinite repetition, is well suited to this sometimes unpleasant task. A higher price of steel scrap, for example, tells thousands of owners and collectors of scrap that more scrap is wanted and that a more exhaustive search for abandoned rails, boilers, radiators, and machines is worth undertaking. A higher price of gasoline tells thousands of automobile drivers that gasoline should be used more sparingly, and the message is repeated each time each driver purchases more gasoline.

THE WORKINGS OF THE PRICE SYSTEM

The complexity and variety of tasks performed by the price system will be illuminated by an examination of three specific economic problems.

THE CHOICE OF OCCUPATION

Individuals must be distributed among occupations in such a way as to serve two basic purposes. First, the labourer must be placed where he is most productive—making certain that Enrico Fermi becomes a physicist rather than a chef and that there are not too many plumbers and too few electricians. Second, the individual worker should be given an occupation that is congenial to him; since he will spend a large part of his life at work, it will be a better life if he can choose the type he prefers.

The price of labour is the instrument by which workers are distributed among occupations: wages in rapidly growing occupations and rapidly growing parts of the nation are higher than in corresponding employment in declining occupations and areas. The choice of occupation involves, however, much more than simply a comparison of wage rates. The following are a few of the complications: (1) The wages of an occupation must as a rule be sufficient to compensate the costs of

Protesters in cities across the United States have advocated for raising the minimum wage to $15 an hour.

training. (2) The wages of an occupation must be sufficient to compensate special disadvantages (such as a large chance of unemployment). (3) Wages must be higher in large cities than in small because living costs are higher in large cities. (4) Wages must compensate workers for their additional skill as they acquire experience (they usually reach a peak of earnings between ages 40 and 55) and thereafter decline as the worker's efficiency declines. (5) Wages will reflect differences in taxation, fringe benefits (pensions, vacations), etc. Accordingly, the wage structure even for a single occupation in a single city is elaborate. When a single wage (price) is imposed upon an occupation, labourers are no longer properly distributed by wages; for example, a city school system that pays all teachers of given experience the same wage finds it difficult to staff its less-attractive schools.

The preferences of the individual worker cannot be given full play, or each person would become president of the corporation at a sumptuous salary. Yet the labourer may choose to live in California rather than Maine; then the price system will incite employers to move their operations to California, where they can hire this labourer more cheaply. The labourer may prefer to work long hours or short hours, and employers are induced by wage offers to cater to the labourer's diverse preferences. In fact, it is equally appropriate to speak of the worker's buying conditions of work and of the employer's buying the services of the worker.

THE CONSERVATION OF RESOURCES

A society has some resources that can be replaced by investment; timber, for example, is now largely grown as a commercial crop. Farmland is a more ancient example: the fertility of soil can be increased by prudent cultivation. Other resources are not replaceable, such as coal and petroleum. How does the price system conserve these exhaustible resources?

The method of using a resource is independent of the pattern over time of income and expenditures that the owner of the resource desires. Suppose that a farm will have a value of $100,000 if it is maintained at a constant level of fertility and yields a yearly income of $10,000 forever but that it can be cultivated ("mined") intensively to yield $12,000 a year for five years at the cost of a much reduced yield thereafter, with a value of $90,000. Even if the farmer is in urgent need of immediate funds and does not expect to live more than five years, he will still cultivate the farm at the uniform rate. Only then is it worth its maximum value to him, and only then (by sale or mortgage) can he obtain the largest-possible funds even in the near future. In short, one need not adapt his expenditure pattern to his income pattern so long as he can borrow or lend.

If the growth of consumption or the decline of reserves threatens the exhaustion of supplies of a resource, then the price of that resource will rise and promise to rise more in the future, and this rise will serve to reduce current consumption and to reward the owner of the resource for holding back much of the supply for the future. This rise in price will therefore also stimulate buyers to find more economical ways of using the commodity (for example, burning the fuel more efficiently) and stimulate producers to find new supplies or substitute products. The price system will therefore ensure that the supply of the resource will be stretched out so that the resource will be available in both the present and the future.

LIMITATIONS AND FAILURES OF THE PRICE SYSTEM

The price system is an extraordinarily powerful instrument in organizing an economic system, but it is subject to three broad classes of limitations.

PRIVATE AND PUBLIC PRICE CONTROL

Sometimes prices are not permitted to do their work. Monopolies are able to exert control over prices, and they use it, sensibly enough, to raise their profits above the level allowed by competition. The monopolist (or group of colluding enterprises) sets prices at a level such that prices are above costs or, to use words of identical significance, such that resources earn more in the monopolized industry than they can earn elsewhere. The basis of the monopoly is its ability to prevent outsiders from entering the industry to share in the unusual profits and, by the act of producing, actually serve to eliminate them.

The fixing of prices by monopolists reduces the income of society. This is, in fact, the only well-established criticism (on grounds of efficiency) to be levied against monopolies; there is no reason to assume that they will make products less-suited to consumer tastes or innovate more slowly or pay lower wages or otherwise misallocate resources. But the basic inefficiency led, first in the United States in 1890 and then increasingly in European nations, to governmental policies to maintain or restore competition.

Public price control has two aspects. A large part of public regulation is intended to correct monopolistic pricing (or other failures of the price system); this includes most public-utility regulation in the United States (transportation, electricity, gas, etc.). Whatever the success of these endeavours—and on the whole there has been a substantial decline in confidence in the regulatory bodies—they are usually instructed to achieve the goals of an efficient price system.

Other public price controls are designed to serve ends outside the reach of the price system. Prices of farm products are regulated (raised) in most nations with the intention of improving farmers' incomes, and the fixing of interest rates paid by banks is undertaken to improve bank earnings. Such policies are invariably defended on various economic and ethical grounds but reflect primarily the political strength of large and well-organized producer groups.

EXTERNALITIES AND THE PRICE SYSTEM

Even when prices are freely established by competition, there is a class of economic relationships called "externalities" not efficiently controlled

EXTERNALITIES

When goods are produced, they may create consequences that no one pays for. Such unaccounted-for consequences are called externalities. Because externalities are not accounted for in the costs and prices of the free market, market agents will receive the wrong signals and allocate resources toward bad externalities and away from good externalities.

Good externalities are consequences that benefit society. However, because those benefits are not accounted for in the price of the good, the price is higher than it should be, and too little of the good is consumed and produced. Bad externalities harm society. However, because the costs of those externalities are not accounted for in the price of the good, the price is lower than it should be, and too much of the good is consumed and produced. In both cases, the market has failed to reach efficiency, because it has allocated resources and production without considering the externalities.

Classic examples of bad externalities include industrial pollution and traffic congestion. Industrial pollution has harmful effects on people and the environment. Yet the cost of producing goods does not include the cost of dealing with the effects of pollution. This means that, in the free market, producers are responding to costs that are too low, and consumers are facing prices that are too low. More goods are produced and sold in the free market than should be, given the negative social effects of pollution.

An example of good externalities is private home renovation. Renovation has a beneficial effect beyond the renovated home, because it increases property values in the neighbourhood. But such benefits are not included in the home owners' calculations in a free market, because their neighbours do not pay them to renovate. As a result, fewer home owners renovate in the free market than the beneficial social effects would justify.

by prices. These may be illustrated by the air pollution caused by automobiles. Since no single automobile makes a significant contribution to air pollution, the owner has no incentive to bear the cost of installing antipollution devices even though all drivers would be better off if each did so. Yet if there are many automobiles in a region, it would be prohibitively expensive for drivers to contract with one another to have each install devices in his automobile to reduce pollution. The external effects of any one automobile's exhaust fumes are so diffuse and affect any one person so triflingly that they cannot be regulated by the price system.

The class of "externalities" is as broad as the class of actions that have effects upon people who are not parties to the contracts governing the actions. An attractive garden pleases passers-by, but they cannot be charged a portion of its cost. A new piece of scientific knowledge will prove useful to unknown persons. These two examples indicate that some externalities are economically trivial and some are highly important.

When the price system cannot deal with diffused effects, other social controls often take its place. The state invokes a whole arsenal of policies to deal with externalities, of which the following are only examples: (1) The state may subsidize activities that do not end in a product that can be sold. Thus, basic scientific research that does not lead to patentable processes is subsidized. (2) Individuals may be compelled to act uniformly in areas where contracts would be too expensive; traffic laws, zoning laws, and compulsory vaccination are examples. (3) The state may itself undertake an activity that cannot be financed by sale of services, the most obvious example being national defense.

An interesting type of externality is the problem of highway congestion. Any one person's presence on a highway at a time and place of peak density has only a negligible effect upon others, so that, except on toll roads, private contracts have not been feasible. The state itself has not been able to deal effectively with highway congestion. More highways can be built until no highway is ever crowded, but this would be intolerably expensive. The state has lacked a method of inducing drivers to shift to less-crowded hours and routes by charging fees to those drivers who impose high congestion costs by driving at peak times. Recent developments in technology have made it feasible to use the price system to reduce congestion. For example, cameras at appropriate points have photographed automobile licenses, and a computer accumulated the charges on the basis of route and time for each automobile. Then only a person for whom travel at peak times was worth, for example, 25 cents per mile would impose (and pay for) the congestion he created.

IMPERFECT KNOWLEDGE AND TASTES

Another limitation to which the price system is subject has to do with the control of knowledge and tastes. To the extent that an economic actor, whether a consumer, a labourer, or an investor, is poorly informed, he is likely to make decisions whose consequences are much different from those he desired and expected. What follows relates only to consumer decisions, but parallel issues arise in labour markets, securities markets, etc.

A consumer can satisfy his desires only if he makes intelligent purchases—that is, only if the goods he buys are what he believes them to be. How can the consumer know whether the meat is free of disease or whether the washing machine will function well and long or whether the fabric of the garment is one synthetic fibre or another? To ascertain these facts personally, the consumer would have to be a versatile scientist equipped with a superb laboratory, and then he would need to spend so much time testing goods that he would have little time to enjoy them.

In some measure the consumer does experiment in his buying: whenever he buys a thing repeatedly, experience tells him much concerning its properties. Direct experience is a sufficient guide in buying celery or hiring domestic servants, but usually the purchase of information takes a less-direct form. The city's premier department store can sell at prices somewhat higher than less-well-known retailers, and the difference represents the payment of a price for reliability, responsibility, and the guarantee of quality. In parallel fashion the consumer buys the washing machine of a company that made his excellent refrigerator. Occasionally, information is bought directly: the advice of a lawyer, the knowledge of an appraiser, the taste of an interior decorator.

The most important and controversial method of informing consumers is by advertising. Many critics are outraged by the self-serving statements of sellers, some of whom indubitably provide irrelevance and deception rather than information. Yet the informational content of advertising may not be as deficient as its critics believe; advertising itself meets two market tests. In the first place, the direct sale of information by consumer advisory services has never become important, although there are no obstacles to entering this business. In the second place, there has been a general, sustained improvement in the quality of consumer goods over time: the automobile tire goes many more miles than formerly; the airplane flies more safely.

Nevertheless, recent public policy has paid great attention to increasing the safety of products and to raising the accuracy of advertising claims.

Knowledge is sometimes difficult to distinguish from taste: does the consumer who persists in smoking cigarettes have inadequate knowledge or simply different comparative values for the pleasures and risks of smoking? Censorship, in any event, is fairly common in every economic system: no society allows young children or incompetents full freedom of action or allows the unlimited sale of narcotics. Since the price system never forbids an effective demand (a demand backed by a willingness to pay the supply price), some form of restriction of prices is therefore necessary if certain tastes are to be forbidden or restricted. Compulsory school attendance can be viewed as, in effect, a form of censorship, and so are the controls on sale of firearms and the taxes on tobacco and liquor.

NONCAPITALIST PRICE SYSTEMS

The foregoing discussion has been confined to the price system as it exists in capitalist economies. Communist countries would have prices, but not autonomous price systems; in those countries the direction of economic activity would largely be in the hands of the central authorities, and prices would be used mainly as accounting devices. None of the four allocative functions of an economy—determination of what will be produced, of how it will be produced, of who will get the product, and of how the product will be distributed—would be performed by the price mechanism in the socialist economies.

The relative scarcities that money prices measure exist, of course, in all countries and would exist in a world where no money or exchanges were allowed. Robinson Crusoe had a problem of allocating his time between sleep, garnering food, building shelter, etc.; and he confronted implicit costs of extending any one activity, because more food meant less of other things. The economist calls these implicit exchange ratios "shadow prices," and they appear in all areas of life in which deliberate choices are made.

Price systems are therefore the result of scarcity. The basic proposition of economics, that scarcities are essentially ubiquitous, is often phrased as "there is no such thing as a free lunch"; and it reminds one that the price of the lunch may be future patronage, a reciprocal lunch, or a boring monologue. The task of economic organization is the task of devising price systems that allow a society to achieve its basic goals.

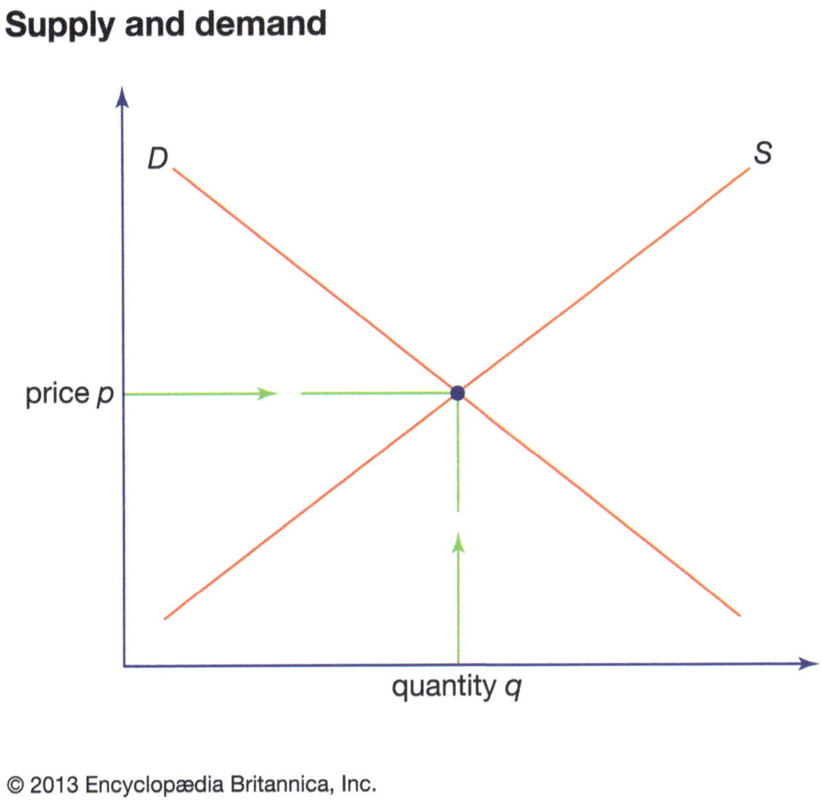

Illustration of the relationship of price (p) to supply (S) and demand (D).

SUPPLY AND DEMAND

One of the most fundamental concepts of economics, supply and demand refers to the relationship between the quantity of a commodity that producers wish to sell at various prices and the quantity that consumers wish to buy. It is the main model of price determination used in economic theory. The price of a commodity is determined by the interaction of supply and demand in a market. The resulting price is referred to as the equilibrium price and represents an agreement between producers and consumers of the good. In equilibrium the quantity of a good supplied by producers equals the quantity demanded by consumers.

DEMAND CURVE

The quantity of a commodity demanded depends on the price of that commodity and potentially on many other factors, such as the prices of other commodities, the incomes and preferences of consumers, and seasonal effects. In basic economic analysis, all factors except

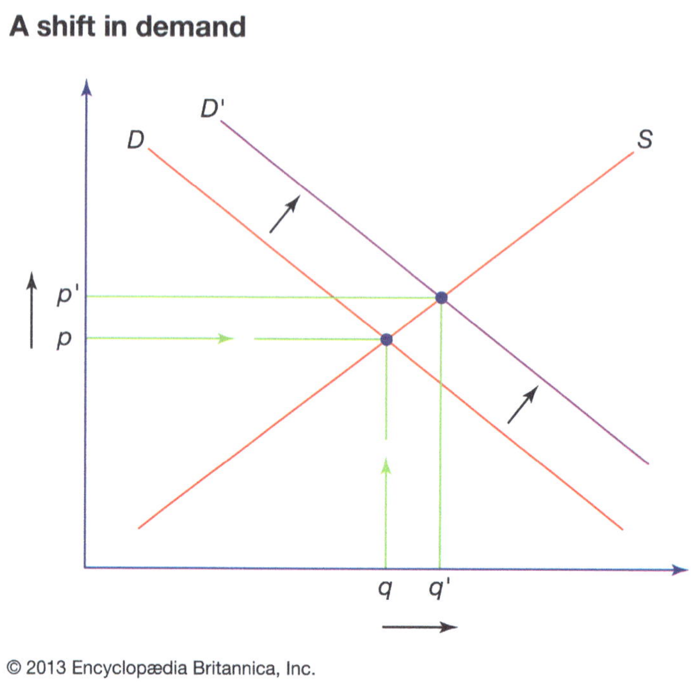

Equilibrium price (p) and equilibrium quantity (q) increase due to a shift in demand (D).

the price of the commodity are often held constant; the analysis then involves examining the relationship between various price levels and the maximum quantity that would potentially be purchased by consumers at each of those prices. The price-quantity combinations may be plotted on a curve, known as a demand curve, with price represented on the vertical axis and quantity represented on the horizontal axis. A demand curve is almost always downward-sloping, reflecting the willingness of consumers to purchase more of the commodity at lower price levels. Any change in non-price factors would cause a shift in the demand curve, whereas changes in the price of the commodity can be traced along a fixed demand curve.

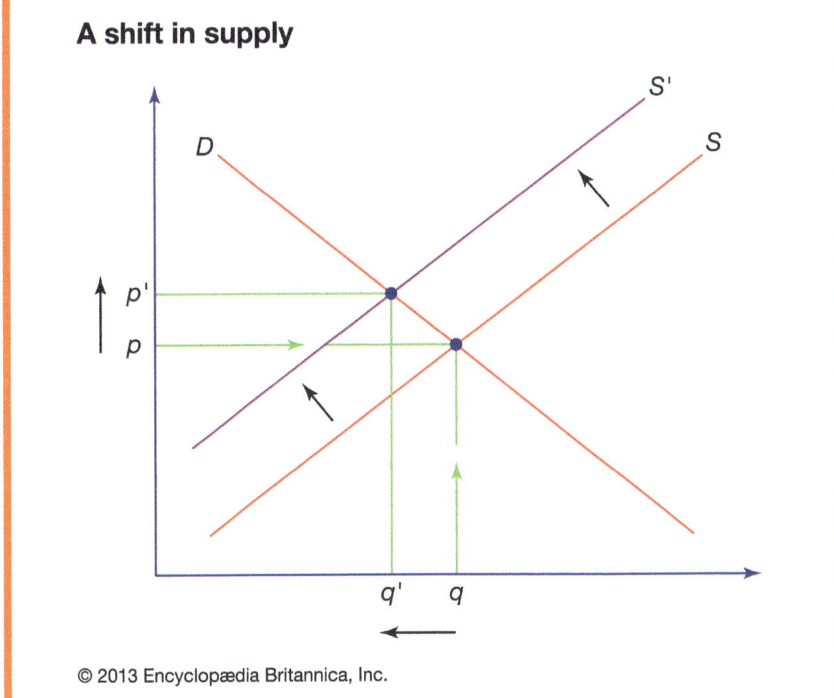

Equilibrium price (p) increases and equilibrium quantity (q) decreases due to a shift in supply (S).

SUPPLY CURVE

The quantity of a commodity that is supplied in the market depends not only on the price obtainable for the commodity but also on potentially many other factors, such as the prices of substitute products, the production technology, and the availability and cost of labour and other factors of production. In basic economic analysis, analyzing supply involves looking at the relationship between various prices and the quantity potentially offered by producers at each price, again holding constant all other factors that could influence the price. Those price-quantity combinations may be plotted on a curve, known as a supply curve, with price represented on the vertical axis and quantity represented on the horizontal axis. A supply curve is usually upward-sloping, reflecting the willingness of producers to sell more of the commodity they produce in a market with higher prices. Any change in non-price factors would cause a shift in the supply curve, whereas changes in the price of the commodity can be traced along a fixed supply curve.

MARKET EQUILIBRIUM

It is the function of a market to equate demand and supply through the price mechanism. If buyers wish to purchase more of a good than is available at the prevailing price, they will tend to bid the price up. If they wish to purchase less than is available at the prevailing price, suppliers will bid prices down. Thus, there is a tendency to move toward the equilibrium price. That tendency is known as the market mechanism, and the resulting balance between supply and demand is called a market equilibrium.

As the price rises, the quantity offered usually increases, and the willingness of consumers to buy a good normally declines, but those changes are not necessarily proportional. The measure of the responsiveness of supply and demand to changes in price is called the price elasticity of supply or demand, calculated as the ratio of the percentage

Elasticity

In economics, elasticity is a measure of the responsiveness of one economic variable to another. A variable *y* (e.g., the demand for a particular good) is elastic with respect to another variable *x* (e.g., the price of the good) if *y* is very responsive to changes in *x*; in contrast, *y* is inelastic with respect to *x* if *y* responds very little (or not at all) to changes in *x*.

Technically, the elasticity of *y* with respect to *x* is calculated as the ratio of the percentage change in the quantity of *y* to the percentage change in the quantity of *x*. In algebraic form, elasticity (E) is defined as E = %Dy/%Dx. *Y* is elastic with respect to *x* if E is greater than 1, inelastic with respect to *x* if E is less than 1, and "unit elastic" with respect to *x* if E is equal to 1.

Elasticity is a very important concept in economics. Several types of elasticities that are frequently used to describe well-known economic variables have acquired their own special names over time. These include, but are not limited to, the price elasticity of supply and demand (the elasticity of supply or demand with respect to price), the income elasticity of demand, the cross-price elasticity (the elasticity of the price of a good with respect to the price of another good), the elasticity of substitution between different factors of production (for example, between capital and labour), and the elasticity of intertemporal substitution (for example, the elasticity of consumption in the future relative to consumption in the present).

change in quantity supplied or demanded to the percentage change in price. Thus, if the price of a commodity decreases by 10 percent and sales of the commodity consequently increase by 20 percent, then the price elasticity of demand for that commodity is said to be 2.

The demand for products that have readily available substitutes is likely to be elastic, which means that it will be more responsive to changes in the price of the product. That is because consumers can easily replace the good with another if its price rises. The demand for a product may be inelastic if there are no close substitutes and if expenditures on the product constitute only a small part of the consumer's income. Firms faced with relatively inelastic demands for their products may increase their total revenue by raising prices; those facing elastic demands cannot.

Supply-and-demand analysis may be applied to markets for final goods and services or to markets for labour, capital, and other factors of production. It can be applied at the level of the firm or the industry or at the aggregate level for the entire economy.

CHAPTER TWO

THE HISTORICAL DEVELOPMENT OF ECONOMICS

The effective birth of economics as a separate discipline may be traced to the year 1776, when the Scottish philosopher Adam Smith published *An Inquiry into the Nature and Causes of the Wealth of Nations*. There was, of course, economics before Smith: the Greeks made significant contributions, as did the medieval scholastics, and from the 15th to the 18th century an enormous amount of pamphlet literature discussed and developed the implications of economic nationalism (a body of thought now known as mercantilism). It was Smith, however, who wrote the first full-scale treatise on economics and, by his magisterial influence, founded what later generations were to call the "English school of classical political economy," known today as classical economics.

THE UNINTENDED EFFECTS OF MARKETS

The *Wealth of Nations*, as its title suggests, is essentially a book about economic development and the policies that can either promote or hinder it. In its practical aspects the book is an attack on the protectionist doctrines of the mercantilists and a brief for the merits of free trade. But in the course of attacking "false doctrines of political economy," Smith

ADAM SMITH

Adam Smith (baptized June 5, 1723, Kirkcaldy, Fife, Scot.—d. July 17, 1790), was a Scottish social philosopher and political economist. In 1737 Smith entered the University of Glasgow and became a student of moral philosophy. Three years later he transferred to Balliol College, Oxford, and remained there until 1746. In 1748 he began delivering a series of public lectures in Edinburgh on wealth and its increase, or as he described it, "the progress of opulence." In 1751 Smith was appointed professor of logic at Glasgow, and the next year he became professor of moral philosophy. His subject matter included ethics, law, rhetoric, and political economy (now called economics). His first book, *The Theory of Moral Sentiments*, was published in 1759. After this book he began to turn his attention toward law and economics. This is evident from student notes taken at his lectures about 1763.

In that year he left Glasgow to become tutor to the duke of Buccleuch, with whom he traveled for two years on the Continent. There he met some of the more prominent theorists in politics and economics, including Jacques Turgot, Jean le Rond d'Alembert, and François Quesnay. Smith then returned home to England and spent most of the next ten years writing his book *An Inquiry into the Nature and Causes of the Wealth of Nations* (1776), the first comprehensive system of political economy. More than two centuries after its publication, he remains a towering figure in the history of economic thought.

Smith is more properly regarded as a social philosopher whose economic writings constitute only the capstone to an overarching view of political and social evolution. If his masterwork is viewed in relation to his earlier lectures on moral philosophy and government, as well as to allusions in *The Theory of Moral Sentiments* (1759) to a work he hoped to write on "the general principles of law and government, and of the different revolutions they have undergone in the different ages and periods of society," then The *Wealth of Nations* may be seen not merely as a treatise on economics but also as a partial exposition of a much larger scheme of historical evolution.

Adam Smith, drawing by John Kay, 1790.

In 1778, two years after the publication of the *Wealth of Nations*, Smith was appointed commissioner of customs and went to live in Edinburgh. He remained there until his death on July 17, 1790.

essentially analyzed the workings of the private enterprise system as a governor of human activity. He observed that in a "commercial society" each individual is driven by self-interest and can exert only a negligible influence on prices. That is, each person takes prices as they come and is free only to vary the quantities bought and sold at the given prices. The sum of all individuals' separate actions, however, is what ultimately determines prices. The "invisible hand" of competition, Smith implied, assures a social result that is independent of individual intentions and thus creates the possibility of an objective science of economic behaviour. Smith believed that he had found, in competitive markets, an instrument capable of converting "private vices" (such as selfishness) into "public virtues" (such as maximum production). But this is true only if the competitive system is embedded in an appropriate legal and institutional framework—an insight that Smith developed at length but that was largely overlooked by later generations. Even so, this is not the only value of the *Wealth of Nations*, and within Smith's discussion of how nations became rich can be found a simple theory of value, a crude theory of distribution, and primitive theories of international trade and of money. Their imperfections notwithstanding, these theories became the building blocks of classical and modern economics. In fact, the book's prolific nature strengthened its impact because so much was left for Smith's followers to clarify.

CONSTRUCTION OF A SYSTEM

One generation after the publication of Smith's tome, David Ricardo wrote *Principles of Political Economy and Taxation* (1817). This book acted, in one sense, as a critical commentary on the *Wealth of Nations*. Yet in another sense, Ricardo's work gave an entirely new twist to the developing science of political economy. Ricardo invented the concept of the economic model—a tightly knit logical apparatus consisting of a few strategic variables—that was capable of yielding, after some manipulation and the addition of a few empirically observable extras, results of enormous practical import. At the heart of the Ricardian system is the notion that economic growth must sooner or later be arrested because of the rising cost of cultivating food on a limited land area. An essential ingredient of this argument is the Malthusian principle—enunciated in Thomas Malthus's *Essay on Population* (1798): according to Malthus, as the labour force increases, extra food to feed the extra mouths can be produced only by extending cultivation to less fertile soil or by applying capital and labour to land already under cultivation—with dwindling results because of the so-called law of diminishing returns. Although wages are held down, profits do not rise proportionately, because tenant farmers outbid each other for superior land. As land prices were increasing, Malthus concluded, the chief beneficiaries of economic progress were the landowners.

Since the root of the problem, according to Ricardo, was the declining yield (i.e., bushels of wheat) per unit of land, one obvious solution was to import cheap wheat from other countries. Eager to show that Britain would benefit from specializing in manufactured goods and exporting them in return for food, Ricardo hit upon the "law of comparative costs" as proof of his model of free trade. He assumed that within a given country labour and capital are free to move in search of the highest returns but that between countries they are not. Ricardo showed that the benefits of international trade are determined by a comparison of costs within each country rather than by a comparison of costs between countries. International trade will profit a country that specializes in the production of the goods it can produce relatively more efficiently (the same country would import everything else). For example, India might be able to produce everything more efficiently than England, but India might profit most by concentrating its resources on textiles, in which its efficiency is relatively greater than in other areas of Indian production, and by importing British capital goods. The beauty of the argument is that if all countries take full advantage of this territorial division of labour, total world output is certain to be physically larger than it will be if some or all countries try to become self-sufficient. Ricardo's law, known as the doctrine of comparative advantage, became the fountainhead of 19th-century free trade doctrine.

The influence of Ricardo's treatise was felt almost as soon as it was published, and for over half a century the Ricardian system dominated economic thinking in Britain. In 1848 John Stuart Mill's restatement of

This 1821 portrait of David Ricardo by Thomas Phillips is in the National Portrait Gallery in London, Eng.

Ricardo's thought in his *Principles of Political Economy* brought it new authority for another generation. After 1870, however, most economists slowly turned away from Ricardo's concerns and began to reexamine the foundations of the theory of value—that is, to explain why goods exchange at the prices that they do. As a result, many of the late 19th-century economists devoted their efforts to the problem of how resources are allocated under conditions of perfect competition.

MARXISM

Before proceeding, it is important to discuss the last of the classical economists, Karl Marx. The first volume of his work *Das Kapital* appeared in 1867; after his death the second and third volumes were published in 1885 and 1894, respectively. If Marx may be called "the last of the classical economists," it is because to a large extent he founded his economics not in the real world but on the teachings of Smith and Ricardo. They had espoused a "labour theory of value," which holds that products exchange roughly in proportion to the labour costs incurred in producing them. Marx worked out all the logical implications of this theory and added to it "the theory of surplus value," which rests on the axiom that human labour alone creates all value and hence constitutes the sole source of profits.

To say that one is a Marxian economist is, in effect, to share the value judgment that it is socially undesirable for some people in the community to derive their income merely from the ownership of property. Since few professional economists in the 19th century accepted this ethical postulate and most were indeed inclined to find some social justification for the existence of private property and the income derived from it, Marxian economics failed to win resounding acceptance among professional economists. The Marxian approach, moreover, culminated in three generalizations about capitalism: the tendency of the rate of profit to fall, the growing impoverishment of the working class, and the

Karl Marx's ideas influenced the economic theories of socialism and communism.

increasing severity of business cycles, with the first being the linchpin of all the others. However, Marx's exposition of the "law of the declining rate of profit" is invalid—both practically and logically (even avid Marxists admit its logical flaws)—and with it all of Marx's other predictions collapse. In addition, Marxian economics had little to say on the practical problems that are the bread and butter of economists in any society, such as the effect of taxes on specific commodities or that of a rise in the rate of interest on the level of total investment. Although Marx's ideas launched social change around the world, the fact remains that Marx had relatively little effect on the development of economics as a social science.

THE MARGINALISTS

The next major development in economic theory, the marginal revolution, stemmed essentially from the work of three men: English logician and economist Stanley Jevons, Austrian economist Carl Menger, and French-born economist Léon Walras. Their contribution to economic theory was the replacement of the labour theory of value with the "marginal utility theory of value." The marginalists based their explanation of prices on the behaviour of consumers in choosing among increments of goods and services; that is, they examined the benefit (utility) that a consumer derives from buying an additional unit of something (a commodity or service) that he already possesses in some quantity. The idea of emphasizing the "marginal" (or last) unit proved in the long run to be more significant than the concept of utility alone, because utility measures only the amount of satisfaction derived from a particular economic activity, such as consumption. Indeed, it was the consistent application of marginalism that marked the true dividing line between classical theory and modern economics. The classical economists identified the major economic problem as predicting the effects of changes in the quantity of capital and labour on the rate of growth of national output. The marginal approach, however, focused on

Marginal Utility

In economics, marginal utility is the additional satisfaction or benefit (utility) that a consumer derives from buying an additional unit of a commodity or service. The concept implies that the utility or benefit to a consumer of an additional unit of a product is inversely related to the number of units of that product he already owns.

Marginal utility can be illustrated by the following example. The marginal utility of one slice of bread offered to a family that has only seven slices will be great, since the family will be that much less hungry and the difference between seven and eight is proportionally significant. An extra slice of bread offered to a family that has 30 slices, however, will have less marginal utility, since the difference between 30 and 31 is proportionally smaller and the family's hunger has been allayed by what it had already. Thus, the marginal utility to a buyer of a product decreases as he purchases more and more of that product, until the point is reached at which he has no need at all of additional units. The marginal utility is then zero.

The concept of marginal utility grew out of attempts by 19th-century economists to analyze and explain the fundamental economic reality of price. These economists believed that price was partly determined by a commodity's utility—that is, the degree to which it satisfies a consumer's needs and desires. This definition of utility, however, led to a paradox when applied to prevailing price relations.

The economists observed that the value of diamonds was far greater than that of bread, even though bread, being essential to the continuation of life, had far greater utility than did diamonds, which were merely ornaments. This problem, known as the paradox of value, was solved by the application of the concept of marginal utility. Because diamonds are scarce and the demand for them was great, the possession of additional units was a high priority. This meant their marginal utility was high, and consumers were willing to pay a comparatively high price for them. Bread is much less valuable only because it is much less scarce, and the buyers of bread possess enough to satisfy their most pressing need for it. Additional purchases of bread beyond people's appetite for it will be of decreasing benefit or utility and will eventually lose all utility beyond the point at which hunger is completely satisfied.

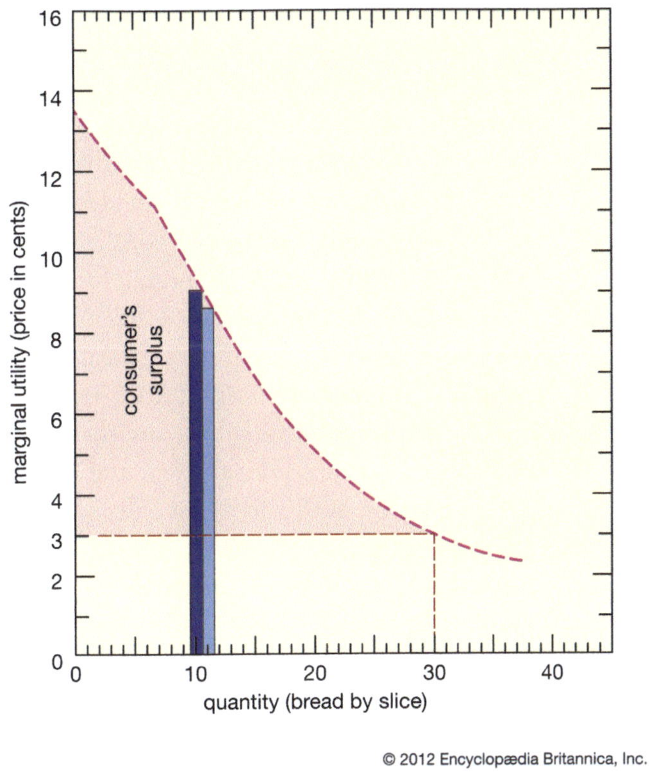

Graph illustrating the inverse relationship between marginal utility and quantity.

The concept of marginal utility was augmented in the 20th century by the method of analysis known as indifference analysis.

the conditions under which these factors tend to be allocated with optimal results among competing uses—optimal in the sense of maximizing consumers' satisfaction.

Through the last three decades of the 19th century, economists of the Austrian, English, and French schools formulated their own interpretations of the marginal revolution. The Austrian school dwelt on the importance of utility as the determinant of value and dismissed classical economics as completely outmoded. Austrian economist Eugen von Böhm-Bawerk applied the new ideas to the determination of the rate of interest, an important development in capital theory.

The English school, led by Alfred Marshall, sought to reconcile their work with the doctrines of the classical writers. Marshall based his argument on the observation that the classical economists concentrated their efforts on the supply side in the market while the marginal utility theorists were concerned with the demand side. In suggesting that prices are determined by both supply and demand, Marshall famously used the paradigm of a pair of scissors, which cuts with both blades. Seeking to be practical, he applied his "partial equilibrium analysis" to particular markets and industries.

It was Léon Walras, though, living in the French-speaking part of Switzerland, who carried the marginalist approach furthest by describing the economic system in general mathematical terms. For each product, he said, there is a "demand function" that expresses the quantities of the product that consumers demand as dependent on its price, the prices of other related goods, the consumers' incomes, and their tastes. For each product there is also a "supply function" that expresses the quantities producers will supply dependent on their costs of production, the prices of productive services, and the level of technical knowledge. In the market, for each product there is a point of "equilibrium"—analogous to the equilibrium of forces in classical mechanics—at which a single price will satisfy both consumers and producers. It is not difficult to analyze the conditions under which equilibrium is possible for a single product. But equilibrium in one market depends on what happens in other markets (a "market" in this sense being not a place or location but a complex array of transactions involving a single good). This is true of every market. And because there are literally millions of markets in a modern economy, "general equilibrium" involves the simultaneous determination of partial equilibria in all markets.

Walras's efforts to describe the economy in this way led the Austrian American Joseph Schumpeter, a historian of economic thought, to call Walras's work "the Magna Carta of economics." While undeniably abstract, Walrasian economics still provides an analytical framework for incorporating all the elements of a complete theory of the economic system. It is not too much to say that nearly the whole of modern economics is Walrasian economics, and modern theories of money, employment, international trade, and economic growth can be seen as Walrasian general equilibrium theories in a highly simplified form.

The years between the publication of Marshall's *Principles of Economics* (1890) and the stock market crash of 1929 may be described as years of reconciliation, consolidation, and refinement for the marginalists. The three schools of marginalist doctrines gradually coalesced into a single mainstream that became known as neoclassical economics. The theory of utility was reduced to an axiomatic system that could be applied to the analysis of consumer behaviour under almost any circumstance. The concept of marginalism in consumption led eventually to the idea of marginal productivity in production, and with it came a new theory of distribution in which wages, profits, interest, and rent were all shown to depend on the "marginal value product" of a factor. Marshall's concept of "external economies and diseconomies" (any external effects, either positive or negative, that a firm or entity might have on people, places, or other markets) was developed by his leading pupil at the University of Cambridge, Arthur Pigou, into a far-reaching distinction between private costs and social costs, thus establishing the basis of welfare theory as a separate branch of economic inquiry. This era also saw a gradual development of monetary theory (which explains how the level of all prices is determined as distinct from the determination of individual prices), notably by Swedish economist Knut Wicksell. In the 1930s the growing harmony and unity of economics was rudely shattered, first by the simultaneous publication of American economist Edward Chamberlin's *Theory of Monopolistic Competition* and British economist Joan Robinson's *Economics of Imperfect Competition* in 1933, then by the appearance of British economist John Maynard Keynes's *General Theory of Employment, Interest and Money* in 1936.

THE CRITICS

Before going on, it is necessary to take note of the rise and fall of the German historical school and the American institutionalist school, which leveled a steady barrage of critical attacks on the orthodox mainstream. The German historical economists, who had many different views, basically rejected the idea of an abstract economics with its supposedly universal laws: They urged the necessity of studying concrete facts in national contexts. While they gave impetus to the study of economic history, they failed to persuade their colleagues that their method was invariably superior.

The institutionalists are more difficult to categorize. Institutional economics, as the term is narrowly understood, refers to a movement in American economic thought associated with such names as Thorstein Veblen, Wesley C. Mitchell, and John R. Commons. These thinkers had little in common aside from their dissatisfaction with orthodox economics, its tendency to cut itself off from the other social sciences, its preoccupation with the automatic market mechanism, and its abstract theorizing. Moreover, they failed to develop a unified theoretical apparatus that would replace or supplement the orthodox theory. This may explain why the phrase *institutional economics* has become little more than a synonym for *descriptive economics*. Particularly in the United States, institutional economics was the dominant style of economic thought during the period between World Wars I and II. At the time there was an expectation that institutional economics would furnish a new interdisciplinary social science. Although there is no longer an institutionalist movement in economics, the spirit of the old institutionalism persists in such best-selling works as Canadian-born economist John Kenneth Galbraith's *The Affluent Society* (1969) and *The New Industrial State* (1967). In addition, there is the "new institutionalism" that links economic behaviour with societal concerns. This school is represented by such scholars as Oliver Williamson and Douglass North, who view institutions as conventions and norms that develop within a market economy to minimize the "transaction costs" of market activity.

It was through the innovations of the 1930s that the theory of monopolist, or imperfect, competition was integrated into neoclassical economics. Nineteenth-century economists had devoted their attention to two extreme types of market structure, either that of "pure monopoly" (in which a single seller controls the entire market for one product) or that of "pure competition" (meaning markets with many sellers, highly informed buyers, and a single, standard product). The theory of monopolistic competition recognized the range of market structures that lie between these extremes, including (1) markets having many sellers with "differentiated products," employing brand names, guarantees, and special packaging that cause consumers to regard the product of each seller as unique, (2) "oligopoly" markets, dominated by a few large firms, and (3) "monopsony" markets, with many sellers but a single monopolistic buyer. The theory produced the powerful conclusion that competitive industries, in which each seller has a partial monopoly because of product differentiation, will tend to have an excessive number of firms, all charging a higher price than they would if the industry were perfectly competitive. Since product differentiation—and the associated phenomenon of advertising—seems to be characteristic of most industries in developed capitalist economies, the new theory was immediately hailed as injecting a healthy dose of realism into orthodox price theory. Unfortunately, its scope was limited, and it failed to provide a satisfactory explanation of price determination under conditions of oligopoly.

This was a significant omission, because in advanced economies most manufacturing and even most service industries are dominated by a few large firms. The resulting gap at the centre of modern price theory shows that economists cannot fully explain the conditions under which multinational firms conduct their affairs.

KEYNESIAN ECONOMICS

The second major breakthrough of the 1930s, the theory of income determination, stemmed primarily from the work of John Maynard Keynes, who asked questions that in some sense had never been posed before. Keynes was interested in the level of national income and the volume of employment rather than in the equilibrium of the firm or the allocation of resources. He was still concerned with the problem of demand and supply, but "demand" in the Keynesian model means the total level of effective demand in the economy, while "supply" means the country's capacity to produce. When effective demand falls short of productive capacity, the result is unemployment and depression; conversely, when demand exceeds the capacity to produce, the result is inflation.

Central to Keynesian economics is an analysis of the determinants of effective demand. The Keynesian model of effective demand consists essentially of three spending streams: consumption expenditures, investment expenditures, and government expenditures, each of which is independently determined. (Foreign trade is ignored.) Keynes attempted to show that the level of effective demand, as determined in this model, may well exceed or fall short of the physical capacity to produce goods and services. He also proved that there is no automatic tendency to produce at a level that results in the full employment of all available human capital and equipment. His findings reversed the assumption that economic systems would automatically tend toward full employment.

By remaining focused on macroeconomic aggregates (such as total consumption and total investment) and by deliberately simplifying the

John Maynard Keynes was one of the most influential economists of the 20th century.

John Maynard Keynes

John Maynard Keynes (b. June 5, 1883, Cambridge, Cambridgeshire, Eng.—d. April 21, 1946, Firle, Sussex), was born into a moderately prosperous family. His father, John Neville Keynes, was an economist and later an academic administrator at the King's College, Cambridge. His mother was one of the first female graduates of the same university, which Keynes entered in 1902.

At Cambridge he was influenced by economist Alfred Marshall, who prompted Keynes to shift his academic interests from mathematics and the classics to politics and economics. Cambridge also introduced Keynes to an important group of writers and artists. The early history of the Bloomsbury group—an exclusive circle of the cultural elect, which counted among its members Leonard and Virginia Woolf, the painter Duncan Grant, and the art critic Clive Bell—centred upon Cambridge and the remarkable figure of Lytton Strachey. Strachey, who had entered Cambridge two years before Keynes, inducted the younger man into the exclusive private club known simply as "the Society." Its members and associates (some of them homosexual, like Keynes himself) were the leading spirits of Bloomsbury. Throughout his life Keynes was to cherish the affection and respond to the influence of this group.

After earning a B.A. in 1905 and an M.A. in 1909, Keynes became a civil servant, taking a job with the India Office in Whitehall. His experience there formed the basis of his first major work, *Indian Currency and Finance* (1913), a definitive examination of pre-World War I Indian finance and currency. He then returned to Cambridge, where he taught economics until 1915. With the onset of World War I, Keynes returned to government employment, this time in the Treasury (an agency even more powerful than its American counterpart), where he studied relations with allies and recommended means of conserving Britain's scant supply of foreign currencies.

Keynes then became a financial consultant in London, where he was regarded as a conventional economist until the depression of the 1930s. In *The General Theory of Employment, Interest and Money* (1936), Keynes departed from his classical theories. He put forth his ideas about government responsibility and commitment to maintaining high employment. He claimed that because consumers were limited in their spending by the size of their incomes, they were not the source of business cycle shifts. The dynamic participants were business investors and governments. The *General Theory*, as it has come to be called, is one of the most influential economics books in history, yet its lack of clarity still causes economists to debate "what Keynes was really saying." He appeared to suggest that a reduction in wage rates would not reduce unemployment; instead, the key to reducing unemployment was to increase government spending and to run a budget deficit. Governments, many of them looking for excuses to increase spending, wholeheartedly accepted Keynes's views. Most of his professional colleagues also accepted his views.

During World War II Keynes played a central role in British war financing and in 1944 was chief British representative at the Bretton Woods Conference that established the International Monetary Fund and the World Bank. His last major public service was his brilliant negotiation in 1945 of a multibillion-dollar loan granted by the United States to Britain. On April 21, 1946, exhausted and overstrained by wartime exertion, Keynes passed away.

relationships between these economic variables, Keynes achieved a powerful model that could be applied to a wide range of practical problems. Others subsequently refined his system of analysis (some have said that Keynes himself would hardly have recognized it), and it became thoroughly assimilated into established economic theory. Still, it is not too much to say that Keynes was perhaps the first economist to have added something truly new to economics since Walras put forth his equilibrium theory in the 1870s.

Keynesian economics as conceived by Keynes was entirely "static"; that is, it did not involve time as an important variable. But one of Keynes's adherents, Roy Harrod, emphasized the importance of time in his simple macroeconomic model of a growing economy. With the publication of *Towards a Dynamic Economics* (1948), Harrod launched an entirely new specialty, "growth theory," which soon absorbed the attention of an increasing number of economists.

POSTWAR DEVELOPMENTS

The 25-year period following World War II can be viewed as an era in which the nature of economics as a discipline was transformed. First of all, mathematics came to permeate virtually every branch of the field. As economists moved from a limited use of differential and integral calculus, matrix algebra represented an attempt to add a quantitative dimension to a general equilibrium model of the economy. Matrix algebra was also associated with the advent of input-output analysis, an empirical method of reducing the technical relations between industries to a manageable system of simultaneous equations. A closely related phenomenon was the development of linear programming and activity analysis, which opened up the possibility of applying numerical solutions to industrial problems. This advance also introduced economists to the mathematics of inequalities (as opposed to exact equation). Likewise, the emergence of growth economics promoted the use of difference and differential equations.

The wider application of mathematical economics was joined by an increasing sophistication of empirical work under the rubric of "econometrics," a field comprising economic theory, mathematical model building, and statistical testing of economic predictions. The development of econometrics had an impact on economics in general, since those who formulated new theories began to cast them in terms that allowed empirical testing.

New developments in economics were not limited to methodological approaches. Interest in the less-developed countries returned in the later decades of the 20th century, especially as economists recognized their long neglect of Adam Smith's "inquiry into the causes of the wealth of nations." There was also a conviction that economic planning was needed to lessen the gap between the rich and poor countries. Out of these concerns came the field of development economics, with offshoots in regional economics, urban economics, and environmental economics.

These postwar developments were best exemplified not by the emergence of new techniques or by additions to the economics curriculum but by the disappearance of divisive "schools," by the increasingly standardized professional training of economists throughout the world, and by the transformation of the science from a rarefied academic exercise into an operational discipline geared to practical advice. This transformation brought prestige (the Nobel Prize in Economic Sciences was first awarded in 1969) but also new responsibility to the profession: now that economics really mattered, economists had to reconcile the differences that so often exist between analytical precision and economic relevance.

RADICAL CRITIQUES

The question of relevance was at the centre of a "radical critique" of economics that developed along with the student revolts and social movements of the late 1960s. The radical critics declared that economics had become a defense of the status quo and that its practitioners had joined the power elite. The marginal techniques of the economists, ran the argument, were profoundly conservative in their bias, because they encouraged a piecemeal rather than a revolutionary approach to social problems; likewise, the tendency in theoretical work to ignore the everyday context of economic activity amounted in practice to the tacit acceptance of prevailing institutions. The critics said that economics should abandon its claim of being a value-free social science and address itself to the great questions of the day—those of civil rights, poverty, imperialism, and environmental pollution—even at the cost of analytical rigour and theoretical elegance.

It is true that the study of economics encourages a belief in reform rather than revolution—yet it must be understood that this is so because economics as a science does not provide enough certitude for any thoroughgoing reconstruction of the social order. It is also true that most economists tend to be deeply suspicious of monopoly in all forms, including state monopolies, and for this reason they tend to favour competition between independent producers as a way of diffusing economic power. Finally, most economists prefer to be silent on large questions if they have nothing to offer beyond the expression of personal preferences. Their greater concern lies in the professional standards of their discipline, and this may mean in some cases frankly conceding that economics has as yet nothing very interesting to say about the larger social questions.

CHAPTER THREE

METHODOLOGICAL CONSIDERATIONS IN CONTEMPORARY ECONOMICS

Economists, like other social scientists, are sometimes confronted with the charge that their discipline is not a science. Human behaviour, it is said, cannot be analyzed with the same objectivity as the behaviour of atoms and molecules. Value judgments, philosophical preconceptions, and ideological biases unavoidably interfere with the attempt to derive conclusions that are independent of the particular economist espousing them. Moreover, there is no realistic laboratory in which economists can test their hypotheses.

In response, economists are wont to distinguish between "positive economics" and "normative economics." Positive economics seeks to establish facts: If butter producers are paid a subsidy, will the price of butter be lowered? Will a rise in wages in the automotive industry reduce the employment of automobile workers? Will the devaluation of currency improve a country's balance of payments? Does monopoly foster technical progress? Normative economics, on the other hand, is concerned not with matters of fact but with questions of policy or of trade-offs between "good" and "bad" effects: Should the goal of price stability be sacrificed to that of full employment? Should income be taxed at a progressive rate? Should there be legislation in favour of competition?

Because positive economics in principle involves no judgments of value, its findings may appear impersonal. This is not to deny that most of the interesting economic propositions involve the addition of definite value judgments to a body of established facts, that ideological bias creeps into the very selection of the questions that economists investigate, or even that much practical economic advice is loaded with concealed value judgments (the better to persuade rather than merely to advise). This is only to say that economists are human. Their commitment to the ideal of value-free positive economics (or to the candid declaration of personal values in normative economics) serves as a defense against the attempts of special interests to bend the science to their own purposes. The best assurance against bias on the part of any particular economist comes from the criticism of other economists. The best protection against special pleading in the name of science is founded in the professional standards of scientists.

METHODS OF INFERENCE

If the science of economics is not based on laboratory experiments (as are the "hard" sciences), then how are facts established? Simply put, facts are established by means of statistical inference. Economists typically begin by describing the terms they believe to be most important in the area under study. Then they construct a "model" of the real world, deliberately repressing some of its features and emphasizing others. Using this model, they abstract, isolate, and simplify, thus imposing a certain order on a theoretical world. They then manipulate the model by a process of logical deduction, arriving eventually at some prediction or implication that is of general significance. At this point, they compare their findings to the real world to see if the prediction is borne out by observed events.

But these observable events are merely a sample, and they may fail to represent real-world examples. This raises a central problem of statistical inference: namely, what can be construed about a population from a sample of the population? Statistical inference may serve as an agreed-upon procedure for making such judgments, but it cannot remove all elements of doubt. Thus the empirical truths of economics are invariably surrounded by a band of uncertainty, and economists therefore make assertions that are "probable" or "likely," or they state propositions with "a certain degree of confidence" because it is unlikely that their findings could have come about by chance.

It follows that judgments are at the heart of both positive and normative economics. It is easy to see, however, that judgments about "degrees of confidence" and "statistical levels of significance" are of a totally different order from those that crop up in normative economics. Normative statements—that individuals should be allowed to spend income as they choose, that people should not be free to control material resources and to employ others, or that governments must offer relief for the victims of economic distress—represent the kind of value judgments associated with the act of disguising personal preferences as scientific conclusions. There is no room for such value judgments in positive economics.

TESTING THEORIES

Most assumptions in economic theory cannot be tested directly. For example, there is the famous assumption of price theory that entrepreneurs strive to maximize profits. Attempts to find out whether they do, by asking them, usually fail; after all, entrepreneurs are no more fully conscious of their own motives than other people are. A logical approach would be to observe entrepreneurs in action. But that would require knowing what sort of action is associated with profit maximizing, which is to say that one would have drawn out all the implications of a profit-maximizing model. Thus one would be testing an assumption about business behaviour by comparing the predictions of a theory of the firm with observations from the real world.

This is not as easy as it sounds. Since the predictions of economics are couched in the nature of probability statements, there can be no such thing as a conclusive, once-and-for-all test of an economic hypothesis. The science of statistics cannot prove any hypothesis; it can only fail to disprove it. Hence economic theories tend to survive until they are falsified repeatedly with new or better data. This is not because they are economic theories but because the attempt to compare predictions with outcomes in the social sciences is always limited by the rules of statistical inference.

It is not remarkable that competing theories exist to explain the same phenomena, with economists disagreeing as to which theory is to be preferred. Much has been written about the uncertain accuracy of economists' predictions. While economists can foretell the effects of specific changes in the economy, they are better at predicting the direction rather than the actual magnitude of events. When economists predict that a tax cut will raise national income, one may be confident that the prediction is accurate; when they predict that it will raise national income by a certain amount in three years, however, the forecast is likely to miss the mark. The reason is that most economic models do not contain any explicit reference to the passage of time and hence have little to say about how long it takes for

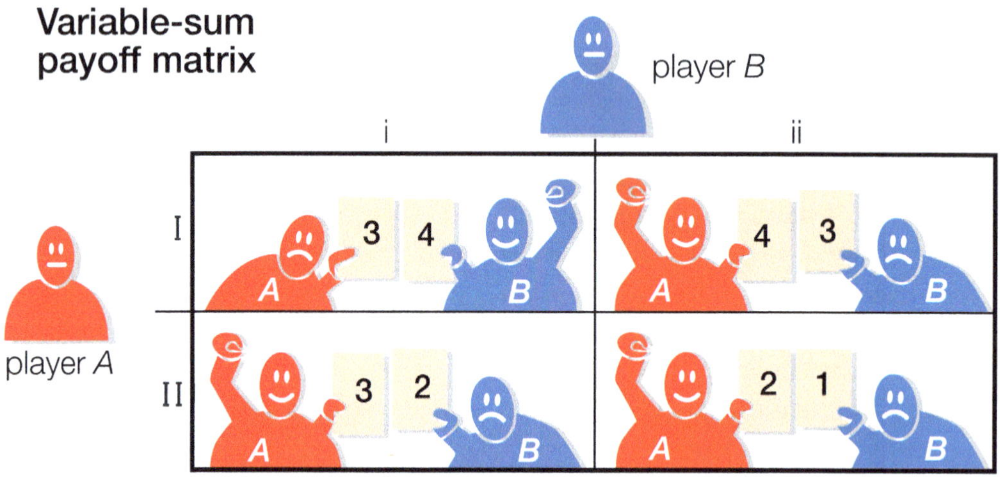

In game theory, a payoff matrix like this shows the different possible outcomes of a hypothetical interaction.

a certain effect to make itself felt. Short-period predictions generally fare better than long-period ones. Since its development in the 1990s, experimental economics has, in fact, been testing economic hypotheses in artificial situations—often by using monetary rewards and student subjects. Much of this innovative work has been stimulated by the ascendance of game theory, the mathematical analysis of strategic interactions between economic agents, represented in such works as *Theory of Games and Economic Behaviour* (1944) by John von Neumann and Oskar Morgenstern. Aspects of game theory have since been applied to nearly every subfield in economics, and its influence has been felt not just in economics but in sociology, political science, and, above all, biology. Because game theory fosters the construction of experimental game situations, it has helped diminish the old accusation that economics is not a laboratory-based discipline.

MICROECONOMICS

Since Keynes, economic theory has been of two kinds: macroeconomics (study of the determinants of national income) and traditional microeconomics, which approaches the economy as if it were made up only of business firms and households (ignoring governments, banks, charities, trade unions, and all other economic institutions) interacting in two kinds of markets—product markets and those for productive services, or factor markets. Households appear as buyers in product markets and as sellers in factor markets, where they offer human labour, machines, and land for sale or hire. Firms appear as sellers in product markets and as buyers in factor markets. In each type of market, price is determined by the interaction of demand and supply; the task of microeconomic theory is to say something meaningful about the forces that shape demand and supply.

Econometrics

Econometrics is the statistical and mathematical analysis of economic relationships, often serving as a basis for economic forecasting. Such information is sometimes used by governments to set economic policy and by private business to aid decisions on prices, inventory, and production. It is used mainly, however, by economists to study relationships between economic variables.

Early econometric studies attempted to quantify the relationship between the price of a commodity and the amount sold. In theory, the demand individual consumers have for particular goods and services will depend on their incomes and on the prices of items they intend to buy. Changes in price and income are expected to affect the total quantity sold.

Early econometricians used market statistics compiled over time to study the relationship between changes in price and demand. Others used family-budget statistics broken down by income level to estimate relationships between income and expenditure. Such studies show which commodities are elastic in demand (i.e., the quantity sold responds to changes in price) and which are inelastic (the quantity sold is less responsive to changes in price).

Consumption patterns, however, are not the only phenomena studied in econometrics. On the producer side, econometric analysis examines production, cost, and supply functions. The production function is a mathematical expression of the technical relationship between a firm's output and its various inputs (or factors of production). The earliest statistical analyses of the production function tested the theory that labour and capital are compensated according to their marginal productivity—i.e., the amount added to production by the "last" worker hired or the "last" unit of capital employed. Later analyses, however, suggest that the wage rate, when adjusted for price changes, is related to labour productivity.

Econometric analysis has refuted some assumptions in cost theory. Work in the field of cost functions, for example, originally tested the theory that marginal cost—the addition to total cost resulting from an increase in output—first declines as production expands but ultimately begins to rise. Econometric studies, however, indicate that marginal cost tends to remain more or less constant.

Work in estimating supply functions has been confined mostly to agriculture. Here the problem is to distinguish the effects of external factors, such as temperature, rainfall, and pestilence, from those of endogenous factors, such as changes in prices and inputs.

After the mid-1930s the development of national income accounting and of macroeconomic theory opened the way for macroeconomic model building, which involved attempts to describe an entire economy in mathematical and statistical terms.

The model developed by L.R. Klein and A.S. Goldberger in the United States after World War II was the forerunner of a large family of macroeconometric models. Constructed on an annual basis, it has been elaborated upon in a form known as the "Michigan model." A later generation of models, based on quarterly data, permits the analysis of short-term movements of the economy and better estimates the lags between different variables.

Continued on page 56

Continued from page 55

A model jointly constructed by the U.S. Federal Reserve Board, the Massachusetts Institute of Technology, and the University of Pennsylvania is specially designed to handle the entire monetary sector. It has a large number of financial equations with a detailed lag structure and supplementary equations to show the main directions of monetary influence on the economy. Similar models have been developed in a number of advanced industrial countries, and many have been constructed for developing economies as well.

A major purpose in the development of macro models has been to improve economic forecasting and the analysis of public policy. Models have also been applied to the analysis of economic fluctuations and economic growth.

THEORY OF CHOICE

Firms face certain technical constraints in producing goods and services, and households have definite preferences for some products over others. It is possible to express the technical constraints facing business firms through a series of production functions, one for each firm. A production function is simply an equation that expresses the fact that a firm's output depends on the quantity of inputs it employs and, in particular, that inputs can be technically combined in different proportions to produce a given level of output. For example, a production engineer could calculate the largest possible output that could be produced with every possible combination of inputs. This calculation would define the range of production possibilities open to a firm, but it cannot predict how much the firm will produce, what mixture of products it will make, or what combination of inputs it will adopt; these depend on the prices of products and the prices of inputs (factors of production), which have yet to be determined. If the firm wants to maximize profits (defined as the difference between the sales value of its output and the cost of its inputs), it will select that combination of inputs that minimizes its expenses and therefore maximizes its revenue. Firms can seek efficiencies through the production function, but production choices depend, in part, on the demand for products. This leads to the part played by households in the system.

Each household is endowed with definite "tastes" that can be expressed in a series of "utility functions." A utility function (an equation similar to the production function) shows that the pleasure or satisfaction households derive from consumption will depend on the products they purchase and on how they consume these products. Utility functions provide a general description of the household's preferences between all the paired alternatives it might confront. Here, too, it is necessary to assume that households seek to maximize satisfaction and that they will distribute their given incomes among available consumer goods in a way that derives the largest possible "utility" from consumption. Their incomes, however, remain to be determined.

In economic theory, the production function contributes to the calculation of supply curves (graphic representations of the relationship between product price and quantity that a seller is willing and able to supply) for firms in product markets and demand curves (graphic representations of the relationship between product price and the quantity of the product demanded) for firms in factor markets. Similarly, the utility function contributes to the calculation of demand curves for households in product markets and the supply curves for households in factor markets. All of these demand and supply curves express the quantities demanded and supplied as a function of prices not because price alone determines economic behaviour but because the purpose is to arrive at a theory of price determination. Much of microeconomic theory is devoted to showing how various production and utility functions, coupled with certain assumptions about behaviour, lead to certain types of demand and supply curves.

Not all demand and supply curves look alike. The essential point, however, is that most demand curves are negatively inclined (consumers demand less as the price rises), while most supply curves are positively inclined (suppliers are likely to produce more at higher prices). The participants in a market will be driven to the price at which the two curves intersect; this price is called the "equilibrium" price or "market-clearing" price because it is the only price at which supply and demand are equal.

For example, in a market for butter, any change—in the production function of dairy farmers; in the utility function of butter consumers; in the prices of cows, grassland, and milking equipment; in the incomes of butter consumers; or in the prices of nondairy products that consumers buy—can be shown to lead to definite changes in the equilibrium price of butter and in the equilibrium quantity of butter produced. Even

Dairy farmers need to be aware of changes in the market that may affect their production and profit.

more predictable are the effects of government-imposed price limits, taxes on butter producers, or price-support programs for dairy farmers, which can be forecast with reasonable certainty. As a rule, the prediction will refer only to the direction of change (the price will go up or down), but if the demand and supply curves of butter can be defined in quantitative terms, one may also be able to foresee the actual magnitude of the change.

THEORY OF ALLOCATION

The analysis of the behaviour of firms and households is to some extent symmetrical: all economic agents are conceived of as ordering a series of attainable positions in terms of an entity they are trying to maximize. A firm aims to maximize its use of input combinations, while a household attempts to maximize product combinations. From the maximizing point of view, some combinations are better than others, and the best combination is called the "optimal" or "efficient" combination. As a rule, the optimal allocation equalizes the returns of the marginal (or last) unit to be transferred between all the possible uses. In the theory of the firm, an optimum allocation of outlays among the factors is the same for all factors; the "law of eventually diminishing marginal utility," a property of a wide range of utility functions, ensures that such an optimum exists. These are merely particular examples of the "equimarginal principle," a tool that can be applied to any decision that involves alternative courses of action. It is not only at the core of the theory of the firm and the theory of consumer behaviour, but it also underlies the theory of money, of capital, and of international trade. In fact, the whole of microeconomics is nothing more than the spelling out of this principle in ever-wider contexts.

The equimarginal principle can be widely applied because economics furnishes a technique for thinking about decisions, regardless of their character and who makes them. Military planners, for example, may consider a variety of weapons in the light of a single objective, damaging an enemy. Some of the weapons are effective against the enemy's army, some against the enemy's navy, and some against the air force; the problem is to find an optimal allocation of the defense budget, one that equalizes the marginal contribution of each type of weapon. But defense departments rarely have a single objective; along with maximizing damage to an enemy, there may be another objective, such as minimizing losses from attacks. In that case, the equimarginal principle will not suffice; it is necessary to know how the department ranks the two objectives in order of importance. The ranking of objectives can be determined through a utility function or a preference function.

When an institution pursues multiple ends, decisions about how to achieve them require a weighting of the ends. Every decision involves a "production function"—a statement of what is technically feasible—and a "utility function"; the equimarginal principle is then invoked to

Gary Becker won a Nobel Prize in Economics for applying economic theory to other social sciences.

Economic Rationality

Economic rationality refers to the various conceptions of rationality used in economic theory. Although there is no single notion of rationality appealed to by all economic theories, there is a core conception that forms the basis of much economic theorizing. That view, termed the *neoclassical conception of economic rationality*, takes rationality to consist primarily of the maximization of subjective utility—that is, the maximal satisfaction of one's own personal desires. Although it is sometimes assumed that subjective utility is equivalent to self-interest (concern for getting one's own wants and needs met exclusive of the effects on others), these are not identical, because the notion of subjective utility allows that one might have preferences that are not purely motivated by self-interest.

The neoclassical conception of economic rationality has been subjected to different criticisms, some of which are ethical in nature. For example, some critics contend that in failing to provide any ethical criterion for the selection of basic goals or ends, economic rationality fails to discriminate between legitimate and illegitimate pursuits on the part of individuals. Without such criteria, some economists consider the theory incomplete but not necessarily false. Other critics note that economists often view economic rationality as a normative concept (that is, it can be applied to a wide variety of people and situations), and economically rational people would thus be required to maximize their individual interests or utility, which could lead them to violate the interests and rights of others. However, not all economists support that view. Some defenders of the neoclassical conception argue that the drive to maximize one's individual interests often leads to cooperation with others and, through the "invisible hand" (the idea that self-interested acts drive social welfare) of the market, to the ultimate common good of all.

provide an efficient, optimal strategy. This principle applies just as well to the running of hospitals, churches, and schools as to the conduct of a business enterprise and is as applicable to the location of an international airport as it is to the design of a development plan for a country. This is why economists advise on activities that are obviously not being conducted for economic reasons. The general application of economics in unfamiliar places is associated with American economist Gary Becker, whose work has been characterized as "economics imperialism" for influencing areas beyond the boundaries of the discipline's traditional concerns. In such books as *An Economic Approach to Human Behavior* (1976) and *A Treatise on the Family* (1981), Becker, who won the Nobel Prize for Economics in 1992, made innovative applications of "rational choice theory." His work in rational choice, which went outside established economic practices to incorporate social phenomena, applied the principle of utility maximization to all decision making and appropriated the notion of determinate equilibrium outcomes to evaluate such noneconomic phenomena as marriage, divorce, the decision to have children, and choices about educating children.

MACROECONOMICS

As stated earlier, macroeconomics is concerned with the aggregate outcome of individual actions. Keynes's "consumption function," for example, which relates aggregate consumption to national income, is not built up from individual consumer behaviour; it is simply an empirical generalization. The focus is on income and expenditure flows rather than the operation of markets. Purchasing power flows through the system—from business investment to consumption—but it flows out of the system in two ways, in the form of personal and business savings. Counterbalancing the savings are investment expenditures, however, in the form of new capital goods, production plants, houses, and so forth. These constitute new injections of purchasing power in

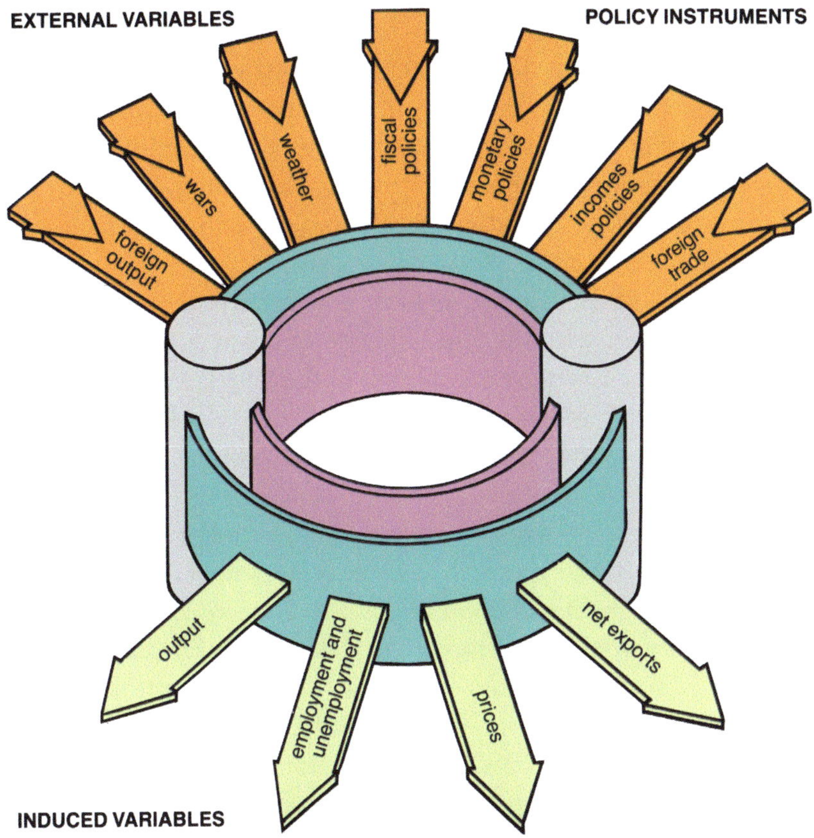

Diagram depicting the components of macroeconomic functioning.

every period. Since savings and investments are carried out by different people for different motives, there is no reason why "leakages" and "injections" should be equal in every period. If they are not equal, national income (the sum of all income payments to the factors of production) will rise or fall in the next period. When planned savings equal planned investment, income will be at an equilibrium level, but when the plans of savers do not match those of investors, the level of income will go on changing until the two do match.

This simple model can take on increasingly complex dimensions by making investment a function of the interest rate or by introducing other variables such as the government budget, the money market, labour markets, imports and exports, or foreign investment. But all this is far removed from the problem of resource allocation and from the maximizing behaviour of individual economic agents, the traditional microeconomic concerns.

The split between macroeconomics and microeconomics—a difference in questions asked and in the style of answers obtained—has continued since the Keynesian revolution in the 1930s. Macroeconomic theory, however, has undergone significant change. The Keynesian system was amplified in the 1950s by the introduction of the Phillips curve, which established an inverse relationship between wage-price inflation and unemployment. At first, this relationship seemed to be so firmly founded as to constitute a virtual "law" in economics. Gradually, however, adverse evidence about the Phillips curve appeared, and in 1968 *The Role of Monetary Policy,* first delivered as Milton Friedman's presidential address to the American Economic Association, introduced the notorious concept of "the natural rate of unemployment" (the minimum rate of unemployment that will prevent businesses from continually raising prices). Friedman's paper defined the essence of the school of economic thought now known as monetarism and marked the end of the Keynesian revolution, because it implied that the full-employment policies of Keynesianism would only succeed in sparking inflation. American economist Robert Lucas carried monetarism one step further: If economic agents were perfectly rational, they would correctly anticipate any effort on the part of governments to increase aggregate demand and adjust their behaviour. This concept of "rational expectations" means that macroeconomic policy measures are ineffective not only in the long run but in the very short run. It was Lucas's concept of "rational expectations" that marked the nadir of Keynesianism, and macroeconomics after the 1970s was never again the consensual corpus of ideas it had been before.

NEOCLASSICAL ECONOMICS

The preceding portrait of microeconomics and macroeconomics is characteristic of the elementary orthodox economics offered in undergraduate courses in the West, often under the heading "neoclassical economics." Given its name by Veblen at the turn of the 20th century, this approach emphasizes

Wal-Mart, the largest retailer in the world, keeps its prices low by using economies of scale.

the way in which firms and individuals maximize their objectives. Only at the graduate level do students encounter the many important economic problems and aspects of economic behaviour that are not caught in the neoclassical net. For example, economics is, first and foremost, the study of competition, but neoclassical economics focuses almost exclusively on one kind of competition—price competition. This focus fails to consider other competitive approaches, such as quantity competition (evidenced by discount stores, such as the American merchandising giant Wal-Mart, that use economies of scale to pass cost savings onto consumers) and quality competition (seen in product innovations and other forms of nonprice competition such as convenient location, better servicing, and faster deliveries). Advertising also plays an important role in the process of competition—in fact, it may be more significant than the competitive strategies of raising or lowering prices, yet standard neoclassical economics has little to say about advertising. The neoclassical approach also tends to ignore the complex nature of business enterprises and the organizational structures that guide effective production. In short, neoclassical economics makes important points about pricing and competition, but in its strictest definition it is not equipped to deal with the varied economic problems of the modern world.

CHAPTER FOUR

FIELDS OF CONTEMPORARY ECONOMICS

Specialized areas of economic investigation attempt to answer questions on a variety of economic activity; they include agricultural economics, economic development, industrial organization, international trade, labour economics, money supply and banking, public finance, information economics, and law and economics. Specialists in mathematical economics and econometrics provide tools used by all economists. The areas of investigation in economics overlap with many other disciplines, notably history, mathematics, political science, and sociology.

MONEY

One of the principal subfields of contemporary economics concerns money, which should not be surprising since one of the oldest, most widely accepted functions of government is control over this basic medium of exchange. The dramatic effects of changes in the quantity of money on the level of prices and the volume of economic activity were recognized and thoroughly analyzed in the 18th century. In the 19th century a tradition developed known as the "quantity theory of money," which held that any change in the supply of money can only be absorbed by variations in the general level of prices (the purchasing power of money). In consequence, prices will tend to change proportionately with the quantity of money in circulation. Simply put, the quantity theory of money stated that inflation or deflation could be controlled by varying the quantity of money in circulation inversely with the level of prices.

One of the targets of Keynes's attack on traditional thinking in his *General Theory of Employment, Interest and Money* (1935–36) was this quantity theory of money. Keynes asserted that the link between the money stock and the level of national income was weak and that the effect of the money supply on prices was virtually nil—at least in economies with heavy unemployment, such as those of the 1930s. He emphasized instead the importance of government budgetary and tax policy and direct control of investment. As a consequence of Keynes's theory, economists came to regard monetary policy as more or less ineffective in controlling the volume of economic activity.

In the 1960s, however, there was a remarkable revival of the older view, at least among a small but growing school of American monetary economists led by Friedman. They argued that the effects of fiscal policy are unreliable unless the quantity of money is regulated at the same time. Basing their work on the old quantity theory of money, they tested the new version on a variety of data for different countries and time periods. They concluded that the quantity of money does matter. *A Monetary History of the United States, 1867–1960*, by Milton Friedman and Anna Schwartz (1963), which became the benchmark work of monetarism, criticized Keynesian fiscal measures along with all other attempts

Milton Friedman won a Nobel Prize in Economics for his work in monetary economics.

at fine-tuning the economy. With its emphasis on money supply, monetarism enjoyed an enormous vogue in the 1970s but faded by the 1990s as economists increasingly adopted an approach that combined the old Keynesian emphasis on fiscal policy with a new understanding of monetary policy.

GROWTH AND DEVELOPMENT

The study of economic growth and development is not a single branch of economics but falls, in fact, into two quite different fields. The two fields—growth and development—employ different methods of analysis and address two distinct types of inquiry.

Development economics is easy to characterize as one of the three major subfields of economics, along with microeconomics and macroeconomics. More specifically, development economics resembles economic history in that it seeks to explain the changes that occur in economic systems over time.

The subject of economic growth is not so easy to characterize. Indeed, it is the most technically demanding field in the whole of modern economics, impossible to grasp for anyone who lacks a command of differential calculus. Its focus is the properties of equilibrium paths, rather than equilibrium states. In applying economic growth theory, one makes a model of the economy and puts it into motion, requiring that the time paths described by the variables be self-sustaining in the sense that they continue to be related to each other in certain characteristic ways. Then one can investigate the way economics might approach and reach these steady-state growth paths from given starting points. Beautiful and frequently surprising theorems have emerged from this experience, but as yet there are no really testable implications nor even definite insights into how economies grow.

Growth theory began with the investigations by Roy Harrod in England and Evsey Domar in the United States. Their independent work, joined in the Harrod-Domar model, is based on natural rates of growth and warranted rates of growth. Keynes had shown that new investment has a multiplier effect on income and that the increased income generates extra savings to match the extra investment, without which the higher income level could not be sustained. One may think of this as being repeated from period to period, remembering that investment, apart from raising income disproportionately, also generates the capacity to produce more output. This results in products that cannot be sold unless there is more demand—that is, more consumption and more investment. This is all there is to the model. It contains one behavioral condition: that people tend to save a certain proportion of extra income, a tendency that can be measured. It also contains one technical condition: that investment generates additional output, a fact that can be established. And it contains one equilibrium condition: that planned saving must equal planned investment in every period if the income level of the period is to be sustained. Given these three conditions, the model generates a time path of income and even indicates what will happen if income falls off the path.

More complex models have since been built, incorporating different saving ratios for different groups in the population, technical conditions for each industry, definite assumptions about the character of technical progress in the economy, monetary and financial equations, and much more. The new growth theory of the 1990s was labeled "endogenous growth theory" because it attempted to explain technical change as the result of profit-motivated research and development (R&D) expenditure by private firms. This was driven by competition along the lines of what Schumpeter called product innovations (as distinct from process innovations). In contrast to the Harrod-Domar model, which viewed growth as exogenous, or coming from outside variables, the endogenous theory emphasizes growth from within the system. This approach enjoyed, and still enjoys, an enormous vogue, partly because it seemed to offer governments a new means of promoting economic growth—namely, national innovation policies designed to stimulate more private and public R&D spending.

PUBLIC FINANCE

Taxation has been a concern of economists since the time of Ricardo. Much interest centres on determining who really pays a tax. If a corporation faced with a profits tax reacts by raising the prices it charges for goods and services, it might succeed in passing the tax on to the consumer. If, however, sales decline as a result of the rise in price, the firm may have to reduce production and lay off some of its workers, meaning that the tax burden has been passed along not only to consumers but to wage earners and shareholders as well.

This simple example shows how complex the so-called "tax incidence" may be. The literature of public finance in the 19th century was devoted to such problems, but Keynesian economics replaced the older emphasis on tax incidence with the analysis of the impact of government expenditures on the level of income and employment. It was some time, however, before economists realized that they lacked a theory of government expenditures—that is, a set of criteria for determining what activities should be supported by governments and what the relative expenditure on each should be. The field of public finance has since attempted to devise such criteria. Decisions on public expenditures have proved to be susceptible to much of the traditional analysis of microeconomics. New developments in the 1960s expanded on a technique known as cost-benefit analysis, which tries to appraise all of the economic costs and benefits, direct and indirect, of a particular activity so as to decide how to distribute a given public budget most effectively between different activities. This technique, first put forth by Jules Dupuit in the 19th century, has been applied to everything from the construction of hydroelectric dams to the control of tuberculosis. Its exponents hoped that the same type of analysis that had proved so fruitful in the past in analyzing individual choice would also succeed with problems of social choice.

Building upon 18th- and 19th-century mathematical studies of the voting process, Scottish economist Duncan Black brought a political dimension to cost-benefit studies. His book *The Theory of Committees and Elections* (1958) became the basis of public choice theory. As expressed in the book *Calculus of Consent* (1962) by American economists James Buchanan and Gordon Tullock, public choice theory applies the cost-benefit analysis seen in private decision making to political decision making. Politicians are conceived of as maximizing electoral votes in the same way that firms seek to maximize profits, while political parties are conceived of as organizing electoral support in the same way that firms organize themselves as cartels or power blocs to lobby governments on their behalf. Public choice challenged the notion, implicit in early public finance theory, that politicians always identify their own interest with that of the country as a whole.

INTERNATIONAL ECONOMICS

Ever since 19th-century economists put forth their theories of international economics, the subject has consisted of two distinct but connected parts: (1) the "pure theory of international trade," which seeks to account for the gains obtained from trade and to explain how these gains are distributed among countries, and (2) the "theory of balance-of-payments adjustments," which analyzes the workings of the foreign exchange market, the effects of alterations in the exchange rate of a currency, and the relations between the balance of payments and level of economic activity.

In modern times, the Ricardian pure theory of international trade was reformulated by American economist Paul Samuelson, improving on the earlier work of two Swedish economists, Eli Heckscher and Bertil

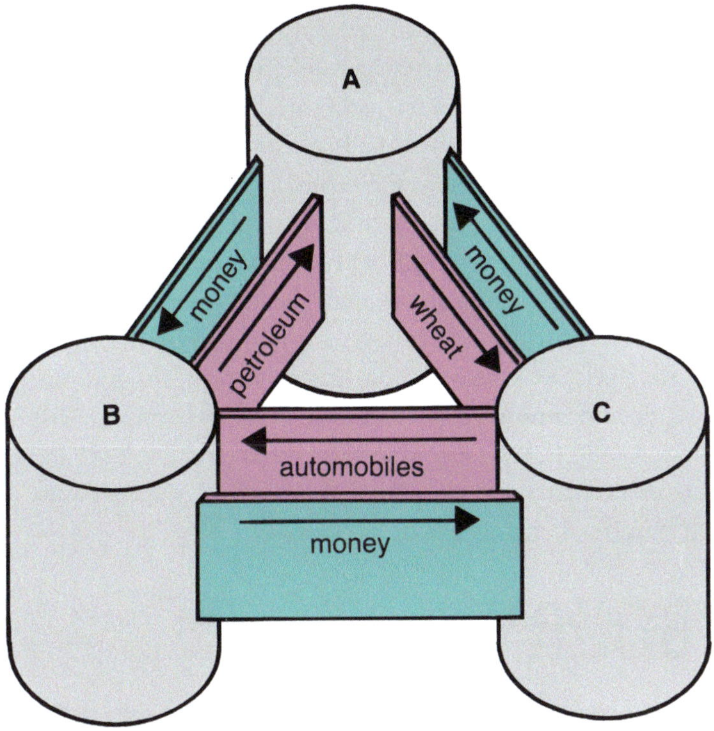

Diagram depicting the relationship between goods, money, and circulating capital.

Ohlin. The so-called Heckscher-Ohlin theory explains the pattern of international trade as determined by the relative land, labour, and capital endowments of countries: A country will tend to have a relative cost advantage when producing goods that maximize the use of its relatively abundant factors of production (thus countries with cheap labour are best suited to export products that require significant amounts of labour).

This theory subsumes Ricardo's law of comparative costs but goes beyond it in linking the pattern of trade to the economic structure of trading nations. It implies that foreign trade is a substitute for international movements of labour and capital, which raises the intriguing question of whether foreign trade may work to equalize the prices of all factors of production in all trading countries. Whatever the answer, the Heckscher-Ohlin theory provides a model for analyzing the effects of a change in trade on the industrial structures of economies and, in particular, on the distribution of income between factors of production. One early study of the Heckscher-Ohlin theory was carried out by Wassily Leontief, a Russian American economist. Leontief observed that the United States was relatively rich with capital. According to the theory, therefore, the United States should have been exporting capital-intensive goods while importing labour-intensive goods. His finding, that U.S. exports were relatively more labour-intensive and imports more capital intensive, became known as the Leontief Paradox because it disputed the Heckscher-Ohlin theory. Recent efforts in international economics have attempted to refine the Heckscher-Ohlin model and test it on a wider range of empirical evidence.

LABOUR

Like monetary and international economics, labour economics is an old economic speciality. Its raison d'être comes from the peculiarities of labour as a commodity. Unlike land or machinery, labour itself is not bought and sold; rather, its services are hired and rented out. But since people cannot be disassociated from their services, various nonmonetary considerations play a concealed role in the sale of labour services.

For many years labour economics was concerned solely with the demand side of the labour market. This one-sided view held that wages were determined by the "marginal productivity of labour"—that is, by the relationships of production and by consumer demand. If the supply of labour came into the picture at all, it was merely to allow for the presence of trade unions. Unions, it was believed, could only raise wages by limiting the supply of labour. Later in the 20th century, the supply side of the labour market attracted the attention of economists, which shifted from the individual worker to the household as a supplier of labour services. The increasing number of married women entering the labour force and the wide disparities and fluctuations observed in the rate that females participate in a labour force drew attention to the fact that an individual's decision to supply labour is strongly related to the size, age structure, and asset holdings of the household to which he or she belongs.

Next, the concept of human capital—that people make capital investments in their children and in themselves in the form of education and training, that they seek better job opportunities, and that they are willing to migrate to other labour markets—has served as a unifying explanation of the diverse activities of households in labour markets. Capital theory has since become the dominant analytical tool of the labour economists, replacing or supplementing the traditional theory of consumer behaviour. The economics of training and education, the economics of information, the economics of migration, the economics of health, and the economics of poverty are some of the by-products of this new perspective. A field that was at one time regarded as rather cut-and-dried has taken on new vitality.

Labour economics, old or new, has always regarded the explanation of wages as its principal task, including the factors determining the general level of wages in an economy and the reasons for wage differentials between industries and occupations. There is no question that wages are influenced by trade unions, and the impact of union activities is of increased importance at a time when governments are concerned with unemployment statistics. Questions of whether prices are being pushed up by the labour unions ("cost push") or pulled up by excess purchasing power ("demand pull") have become the issues in the larger debate on inflation—a controversy that is directly related to the debates in monetary economics mentioned earlier.

INDUSTRIAL ORGANIZATION

The principal concerns of industrial organization are the structure of markets, public policy toward monopoly, the regulation of public utilities, and the economics of technical change. The monopoly problem, or, more precisely, the problem of the maintenance of competition, does not fit well into the received body of economic thought. Economics started out, after all, as the theory of competitive enterprise, and even today its most impressive theorems require the assumption of numerous small firms, each having a negligible influence on price. Yet, as noted earlier, contemporary market structures tend toward oligopoly—competition among the few—with some industries dominated by firms so large their annual sales volume exceeds the national income of the smaller European countries. It is tempting to conclude that oligopoly is so deleterious to economic welfare on the ground that it leads to the misallocation of resources. But some economists, notably Schumpeter, have argued that economic growth and technical progress are achieved not through free competition

The communications industry is an example of an oligopoly; Time Warner is one of the few major companies.

but by the enlargement of firms and the destruction of competition. According to this view, the giant firms compete not in price but in successful innovation, and this kind of competition has proved more effective for economic progress than the more traditional price competition.

This thesis makes somewhat less compelling the merits of "trust busting," largely taken for granted since the administration of U.S. Pres. Theodore Roosevelt first set about curbing the concentration of corporate power in the early 20th century. Instead, it points the way for a consideration of competition that seeks to attain the greatest benefit for society. For example, if four or five large firms in an oligopolistic industry compete on the basis of product quality, research, technology, or merchandising, the performance of the entire industry may well be more satisfactory than if it were reorganized into a price-competitive industry. But if the four or five giants compete only in sales promotion techniques, the outcome will likely be less favourable for society. One cannot, therefore, draw facile conclusions about the competitive results of different market structures.

Much uncertainty in the economic discussion of policies towards big business stems from the lack of a general theory of oligopoly. Perhaps

Perfect Competition

Market conduct and performance in atomistic industries provide standards against which to measure behaviour in other types of industry. The atomistic category includes both perfect competition (also known as pure competition) and monopolistic competition. In perfect competition, a large number of small sellers supply a homogeneous product to a common buying market.

Continued on page 78

Continued from page 77

In this situation no individual seller can perceptibly influence the market price at which he sells but must accept a market price that is impersonally determined by the total supply of the product offered by all sellers and the total demand for the product of all buyers. The large number of sellers precludes the possibility of a common agreement among them, and each must therefore act independently. At any going market price, each seller tends to adjust his output to match the quantity that will yield him the largest aggregate profit, assuming that the market price will not change as a result. But the collective effect of such adjustments by all sellers will cause the total supply in the market to change significantly, so that the market price falls or rises. Theoretically, the process will go on until a market price is reached at which the total output that sellers wish to produce is equal to the total output that all buyers wish to purchase. This way of reaching a provisional equilibrium price is what the Scottish economist and philosopher Adam Smith described when he wrote of prices being determined by "the invisible hand" of the market.

If the provisional equilibrium price is high enough to allow the established sellers profits in excess of a normal interest return on investment, then added sellers will be drawn to enter the industry, and supply will increase until a final equilibrium price is reached that is equal to the minimal average cost of production (including an interest return) of all sellers. Conversely, if the provisional equilibrium price is so low that established sellers incur losses, some will withdraw from the industry, causing supply to decline until the same sort of long-run equilibrium price is reached.

The long-run performance of a purely competitive industry therefore embodies these features: (1) industry output is at a feasible maximum and industry selling price at a feasible minimum; (2) all production is undertaken at minimum attainable average costs, since competition forces them down; and (3) income distribution is not influenced by the receipt of any excess profits by sellers.

This performance has often been applauded as ideal from the standpoint of general economic welfare. But the applause, for several reasons, should not be unqualified. Perfect competition is truly ideal only if all or most industries in the economy are purely competitive and if in addition there is free and easy mobility of productive factors among industries. Otherwise, the relative outputs of different industries will not be such as to maximize consumer satisfaction. There is also some question whether producers in purely competitive industries will generally earn enough to plow back some of their earnings into improved equipment and thus maintain a satisfactory rate of technological progress. Innovation would effectively be discouraged. Finally, some purely competitive industries have been afflicted with what has been called destructive competition. Examples have been seen in the coal and steel industries, some agricultural industries, and the automotive industry. For some historical reason, such an industry accumulates excess capacity to the point where sellers suffer chronic losses, and the situation is not corrected by the exit of people and resources from the industry. The invisible hand of the market works too slowly for society to accept. In some cases, notably in agriculture, government has intervened to restrict supply or raise prices. Leaving these qualifications aside, however, the market performance of perfect competition furnishes some sort of a standard to which the performance of industries of different structure may be compared.

a loose criterion for judging the desirability of different market structures is American economist William Baumol's concept of "contestable markets": If a market is easy to enter and to exit, it is "contestable" and hence workably competitive.

AGRICULTURE

Farming has long provided economists with their favourite example of a perfectly competitive industry. However, given the level of government regulation of and support for agriculture in most countries, farming also provides striking examples of the effects of price controls, income supports, output ceilings, and marketing cartels. Not surprisingly, agricultural economics commands attention wherever governments wish to stimulate farming or to protect farmers—which is to say everywhere.

Agricultural economists generally have been closer to their subject matter than other economists. In consequence, more is known about the technology of agriculture, the nature of farming costs, and the demand for agricultural goods than is known about any other industry. Thus the field of agricultural economics offers a rich literature on the basics of economic study, such as estimating a production function or plotting a demand curve.

LAW AND ECONOMICS

One of the most remarkable new developments is the growth of a discipline combining legal and economic concerns. Its origins in the 1970s are almost wholly due to the unintended effects of two articles by Ronald Coase, a British economist specializing in industrial organization. Before emigrating to the United States in 1950, Coase published *The Nature of the Firm* (1937), which was the first paper to pose a seemingly innocent question: Why are there firms at all—why not a collection of independent producers and merchants supplying whatever is called for in the market? Firms are, after all, nonmarket administrative organizations. Coase determined that firms spring up to minimize the "transaction costs" of marketing—namely, the costs of drawing up contracts and monitoring their implementation. Coase's idea—that all economic transactions are in fact explicit or implicit contracts and hence that the role of the law in enforcing contracts is crucial to the operations of a market economy—was soon seen as a revelation. Economic institutions (such as corporations) came to be viewed as social devices for reducing transaction costs.

Coase contributed yet another central tenet of law and economics as a unified field of study in his paper *The Problem of Social Cost* (1960). Here he argued that, except for transaction costs, not only could private deals between voluntary agents always accommodate market failures but that "government failures" (that is, those caused by government intervention) were as deleterious as market failures, if not more so. As Coase stated in the paper,

> **Direct governmental regulation will not necessarily give better results than leaving the problem to be solved by the market or firm. But equally, there is no reason why on occasion such governmental administrative regulation should not lead to an improvement in economic efficiency.**

In other words, transaction costs were central to the problem of social welfare, and markets were inherently more efficient than any social intervention devised by governments. Up to this point the accepted neoclassical welfare economics had promoted "perfect competition" as the best of all possible economic worlds. This theoretical market structure comprised a world of many small firms whose product prices were determined by the sum of all their output decisions in relation to the independent demand of consumers. This perfect condition, however, depended on increasing returns to scale that allow firms to cut costs as their businesses expand. The concept of perfect competition therefore assumed that one or more of the small firms must fail. This argument has been known ever since as the Coase theorem, and "The Problem of Social Cost" produced not just law and economics as a speciality study in economics but led to the new institutionalism in industrial organization referred to earlier.

INFORMATION ECONOMICS

Toward the end of the 20th century, information economics became an increasingly important specialization. It is almost wholly the legacy of a single article entitled *The Market for 'Lemons': Quality Uncertainty and the Market Mechanism* by George Akerlof (1970). Akerlof asserted that the market for secondhand cars is one in which sellers know much more than buyers about the quality of the product being sold, implying that only the worst cars—"lemons"—reach the secondhand car market. As a result, secondhand-car dealers are compelled to offer guarantees as a means of increasing their customers' confidence. A buyer who knows more about a transaction (i.e., the quality of the secondhand car) will be willing to pay more than a buyer who is provided less information about a transaction. For any product or service, therefore, "asymmetric information" (one party to a transaction knowing more than another) can result in "missing markets," or the absence of a marketable transaction. The potency of this idea and its relevance to all sorts of economic behaviour captivated many economists, leading some to connect it with contract theory and principal-agency theory (concerning situations in which a principal hires an agent to carry out instructions but then has to monitor the agent's performance, as in franchising a business). Two or three decades after Akerlof's groundbreaking work, it was abundantly clear that information economics flowed from his underlying idea of asymmetric information, and in 2001 Akerlof, Joseph Stiglitz, and Michael Spence were jointly awarded the Nobel Prize in Economics for their work in this area.

FINANCIAL ECONOMICS

Although news about the stock market has come to dominate financial journalism, only since the late 20th century was the stock market recognized as an institution suitable for economic analysis. This recognition turned on a changed understanding of the "efficient market hypothesis," which held that securities prices in an efficient stock market were inherently unpredictable—that is, an investment in the stock market was, for all but insider traders, equivalent to gambling in a casino. (An efficient stock market was one in which all information relevant to the discounted present value of stocks was freely available to all participants in the market and hence was immediately incorporated into their buying and selling plans; stock market prices were unpredictable because every fact that made them predictable had already been acted on.) In the famous economists' joke, there is no point in picking up a $10 bill lying on the sidewalk, because if it were real, someone else would already have picked it up.

The growth of financial markets, the deregulation of international capital markets, and the unprecedented availability of financial data gradually undermined the efficient market hypothesis. By the 1990s there had been enough "bubbles" in stock prices to remind economists of the excessive volatility of stock markets (and to prompt Federal Reserve Board chairman Alan Greenspan to point to the market's "irrational exuberance" when share prices hit new peaks late in the decade). The securities markets seemed anything but efficient. In any case, finance is an area where facts can be highly ambiguous but the number of people desperately interested in the nature of those facts will guarantee the further growth of financial economics.

Though most stock trading is now electronic, there are still traders on the floor of the New York Stock Exchange.

OTHER SCHOOLS AND FIELDS OF ECONOMICS

There are different schools of thought in economics, each with its own journals and conferences. One, the Austrian school, now rooted in the United States, with leading centres at New York University and George Mason University, originated in the works of Carl Menger, Friedrich von Wieser, and Böhm-Bawerk, all of whom emphasized utility as a component of value. Its free market precepts were brought to the United

States by Ludwig Mises and the well-known author of *The Road to Serfdom* (1944), Friedrich A. Hayek.

Charles Darwin's influence can be seen in all of the social sciences, and another alternative school, evolutionary economics—like much of the literature in economics, psychology, and sociology—builds on analogies to evolutionary processes. Also drawing heavily on game theory, it is primarily concerned with economic change, innovation, and dynamic competition. This is not, of course, the first time that economists have flirted with Darwinian biology. Both Veblen and Alfred Marshall were convinced that biology and not mechanics offered the road to theoretical progress in economics, and, while this belief in biological thinking died out in the early years of the 20th century, it has returned to prominence in evolutionary economics.

Pairing his critique of central planning with a defence of free markets, Hayek became a sophisticated evolutionary economist whose advocacy of markets drew attention to the weakest element in mainstream economics: the assumption that economic agents are always perfectly informed of alternative opportunities. A follower of Mises and Hayek, American economist Israel Kirzner developed this line of thinking into a unique Austrian theory of entrepreneurship (involving spontaneous learning and decision making at the individual level) that emphasized a tendency toward economic equilibrium.

Yet another school outside the mainstream is Sraffian economics. As an offshoot of general equilibrium theory, Sraffian economics purports to explain the determination of prices by means of the technological relationships between inputs and outputs without invoking the preferences of consumers that neoclassical economists rely on so heavily. Moreover, Sraffian theory is said to recover the classical economic tradition of Smith and Ricardo, which Sraffians believe has been deliberately buried by neoclassical orthodoxy. All of this stems from Piero Sraffa's *The Production of Commodities by Means of Commodities* (1962), whose 100 or so pages have attracted thousands of pages of elucidation, though the true meaning of Sraffian economics still remains somewhat elusive.

AUSTRIAN SCHOOL OF ECONOMICS

The Austrian School of Economics refers to the body of economic theory developed in the late 19th century by Austrian economists who, in determining the value of a product, emphasized the importance of its utility to the consumer. Carl Menger published the new theory of value in 1871, the same year in which English economist William Stanley Jevons independently published a similar theory.

Menger believed that value is completely subjective: a product's value is found in its ability to satisfy human wants. Moreover, the actual value depends on the product's utility in its least important use. If the product exists in abundance, it will be used in less-important ways. As the product becomes more scarce, however, the less-important uses are abandoned, and greater utility will be derived from the new least-important use. (This idea relates to one of the most important laws in economics, the law of demand, which says that when the price of something rises, people will demand less of it.)

This theory of value also supplies an answer to the so-called "diamond-water paradox," which economist Adam Smith pondered but was unable to solve. Smith noted that, even though life cannot exist without water and can easily exist without diamonds, diamonds are, pound for pound, vastly more valuable than water. The marginal-utility theory of value resolves the paradox. Water in total is much more valuable than diamonds in total because the first few units of water are necessary for life itself. But, because water is plentiful and diamonds are scarce, the marginal value of a pound of diamonds exceeds the marginal value of a pound of water. The idea that value derives from utility contradicted Karl Marx's labour theory of value, which held that an item's value derives from the labour used to produce it and not from its ability to satisfy human wants.

The theory of marginal utility was applied to production as well as to consumption. Friedrich von Wieser based the value of productive resources on their contribution to the final product, recognizing that changes in the amount used of one productive factor would alter the productivity of other factors. He also introduced the concept of opportunity cost: Wieser showed that the cost of a factor of production can be determined by its utility in some alternative use—i.e., an opportunity forgone. The concept of "opportunity cost," as identified by Wieser, is still widely used in modern economic analysis.

Eugen von Böhm-Bawerk developed marginal-utility analysis into a theory of price. Böhm-Bawerk is best known, however, for his work on capital and interest, in which he emphasized the role of time in determining the value of goods. He viewed interest as the charge for the use of capital—a compensation to the owner for abstaining from present consumption. The rate of interest was determined by the size of the labour force, the amount of a community's capital, and the possibility of increasing productivity through methods of production.

The two leading Austrian economists of the 20th century were Ludwig von Mises and Friedrich A. Hayek. Mises (in the 1920s) and Hayek (in the 1940s) both showed that a complex economy cannot be rationally planned because true market prices are absent. As a result, the information critical for centralized planning cannot be obtained.

Be that as it may, Sraffian economics is a good example of the unequal global diffusion of economic specialization; while it is recognized as a minority school of thought in Europe, Sraffian economics is virtually unknown in American academic circles.

Radical economics, including feminist economics, is better characterized by what it opposes than by what it advocates. A glance at the pages of the *Review of Radical Political Economics* and *Feminist Economics* may cause some to wonder if these specialized concerns should even be considered as economics. That question leads back to the notion that economics is what economists do; in that light, heterodox economics, as exemplified by these and similar networks of dissenters, is indeed economics.

Other principal fields in economics include economic history, health economics, cultural economics, economics of education, demographic economics, the study of nonprofit organizations, economic regulation, business management, comparative economic systems, environmental economics, urban and regional economics, and spatial economics.

Economics has always been taught in conjunction with economic history, but the relationship between these two fields has never been an easy one, and to this day economics departments in the United States include economic historians. In most of Europe, however, economists and economic historians are not joined together institutionally. Although economic historians have won Nobel Prizes (Simon Kuznets in 1971, and Robert Fogel and Douglass North in 1993), most economists do not aspire to study in this area.

The growth of public interest in certain areas affects economists as much as other people. It is not surprising therefore that environmental economics has been an emerging subfield of economics. Marshall and his principal student, Arthur Pigou, created the subject of welfare economics around the theme of the negative "externalities" or spillovers (such as pollution) caused by the growth of big business. Should such "diseconomies of scale" be controlled by administrative regulation, or should firms be made to pay for them by selling them licenses to pollute?

Air pollution is among the negative externalities studied by environmental economists.

Global warming has dramatized the importance of these questions, and the concerns of environmental economics were priorities of applied economists at the start of the 21st century.

In the 1960s the American "war on poverty" and concerns about schooling brought the economics of education to the fore. That was the decade of interest in human capital theory, and since then the growing health bill of Western countries has drawn similar attention to health economics as a specialization. This is unlikely to change in the years to come, and health economics is perhaps the field in the applied economics of the future with the most promising potential. One might have thought that the same would apply to spatial economics or the economics of location. After all, what could be more important than the location at which economic activity is carried out? How can the marketing of products be studied without paying attention to the role of location? But although spatial economics has a long and rich history of scholarship (including the work of Johann Heinrich von Thünen and Alfred Weber), it has never attracted the steady interest of economists. Why that is so is a big unanswered question.

Lastly, there is the influence from the field of business management. Developments in higher education have fostered the study of economics within business schools (as opposed to maintaining distinct departments of economics). This trend has been encouraged by the institutions that hire new economists, such as banks, brokerage firms, and governments. As a result, many colleges and universities have reduced their economics faculties while building up their management faculties. The fields of business administration and business economics have their own gurus, but only a few (such as American economists Herbert Simon and Alfred Chandler) straddle both economics and management. By and large, these are different worlds, and only time will tell whether economics and management will one day merge into some new, more comprehensive subject in the study of business governance. What is certain is that economics will remain a vital branch of knowledge, as central to curricula of universities as it is to the conduct of human interaction, with an ongoing proliferation of new theories, schools, and subfields.

CHAPTER FIVE

THE EVOLUTION OF ECONOMIC SYSTEMS: PREHISTORY TO CAPITALISM

Humankind has arranged for its material provisioning through economic systems. One would think that there would be a great variety of such systems, corresponding to the many cultural arrangements that have characterized human society. Surprisingly, that is not the case. Although a wide range of institutions and social customs have been associated with the economic activities of society, only a very small number of basic modes of provisioning can be discovered beneath this variety. Indeed, history has produced but three such kinds of economic systems: those based on the principle of tradition, those centrally planned and organized according to command, and the rather small number, historically speaking, in which the central organizing form is the market.

The very paucity of fundamental modes of economic organization calls attention to a central aspect of the problem of economic "systems"—namely, that the objective to which all economic arrangements must be addressed has itself remained unchanged throughout human history. Simply stated, this unvarying objective is the coordination of the individual activities associated with provisioning—activities that range from providing subsistence foods in hunting and gathering societies to administrative or financial tasks in modern industrial systems. What may be called "the economic problem" is the orchestration of these activities into a coherent social whole—coherent in the sense of providing a social order with the goods or services it requires to ensure its own continuance and to fulfill its perceived historic mission.

Social coordination can in turn be analyzed as two distinct tasks. The first of these is the production of the goods and services needed by the social order, a task that requires the mobilization of society's resources, including its most valuable, human effort. Of nearly equal importance is the second task, the appropriate distribution of the product. This distribution not only must provide for the continuance of a society's labour supply (even slaves had to be fed) but also must accord with the prevailing values of different social orders, all of which favour some recipients of income over others—men over women, aristocrats over commoners, property owners over non-owners, or political party members over nonmembers. In standard textbook treatments, the economic problem of production and distribution is summarized by three questions that all economic systems must answer: what goods and services are to be produced, how goods and services are to be produced and distributed, and for whom the goods and services are to be produced and distributed.

All modes of accomplishing these basic tasks of production and distribution rely on social rewards or penalties of one kind or another. Tradition-based societies depend largely on communal expressions of approval or disapproval. Command systems utilize the open or veiled power of physical coercion or punishment, or the bestowal of wealth or prerogatives. The third mode—the market economy—also brings pressures and incentives to bear, but the stimuli of gain and loss are not usually within the control of any one person or group of persons. Instead, the incentives and pressures emerge from the "workings" of the system itself, and, on closer inspection, those workings turn out to be nothing other than the efforts of individuals to gain financial rewards by supplying the things that others are willing to pay for.

There is a paradoxical aspect to the manner in which the market resolves the economic problem. In contrast to the conformity that guides traditional society or the obedience to superiors that orchestrates command society, behaviour in a market society is mostly self-directed and seems, accordingly, an unlikely means for achieving social integration. Yet, as economists ever since Adam Smith have delighted in pointing out, the clash of self-directed wills in the competitive market environment serves as an essential legal and social precondition for the market system to operate. Thus, the competitive engagement of self-seeking individuals results in the creation of the third, and by all odds the most remarkable, of the three modes of solving the economic problem.

Not surprisingly, these three principal solutions—of tradition, command, and market—are distinguished by the distinct attributes they impart to their respective societies. The coordinative mechanism of tradition, resting as it does on the perpetuation of social roles, is marked by a characteristic changelessness in the societies in which it is dominant. Command systems, on the other hand, are marked by their capacity to mobilize resources and labour quickly and on a national scale. Such coordination, generally unattainable by traditional societies, engendered such large-scale achievements as the Great Wall of China and the Egyptian pyramids. The third system, that in which the market mechanism plays the role of energizer and coordinator, is in turn marked by a historical attribute that resembles neither the routines of traditional systems nor the grandiose products of command systems. Instead, the market system imparts a galvanic charge to economic life by unleashing competitive, gain-oriented energies. This charge is dramatically illustrated by the trajectory of capitalism, the only social order in which the market mechanism has played a central role. In *The Communist Manifesto*, published in 1848, Karl Marx and Friedrich Engels wrote that in less than a century the capitalist system had created "more massive and more colossal productive forces than have all preceding generations together." They also wrote that it was "like the sorcerer, who is no longer able to control the powers of the nether world whom he has called up by his spells." That creative, revolutionary, and sometimes disruptive capacity of capitalism can be traced in no small degree to the market system that performs its coordinative task.

PREHISTORIC AND PRELITERATE ECONOMIC SYSTEMS

Although economics is primarily concerned with the modus operandi of the market mechanism, an overview of premarket coordinative arrangements not only is interesting in itself but throws a useful light on the distinctive properties of market-run societies.

The earliest and by far the most historically numerous of economic systems has been that of primitive society, for which tradition serves as the central means of bestowing order. Such economic forms of social organization are likely to be far more ancient than Cro-Magnon people, although a few of these forms are still preserved by such groups as the Eskimo, Kalahari hunters, and Bedouin. So far as is known, all tradition-bound peoples solve their economic problems today much as they did 10,000 years or perhaps 10,000 centuries ago—adapting by migration or movement to changes in season or climate, sustaining themselves by hunting and gathering or by slash-and-burn agriculture, and distributing their output by reference to well-defined social claims. Elizabeth Marshall Thomas describes this distributive system in *The Harmless People* (1958):

> **It seems very unequal when you watch Bushmen divide the kill, yet it is their system, and in the end no person eats more than the other. That day Ukwane gave Gai still another piece because Gai was his relation, Gai gave meat to Dasina because she was his wife's mother....No one, of course, contested Gai's large share, because he had been the hunter.... No one doubted that he would share his large amount with others, and they were not wrong, of course; he did.**

A group of hunter-gatherers who are part of the San people, or Bushmen, share a meal.

Besides the shared property that is perhaps the outstanding attribute of these hunting and gathering societies, two further aspects deserve attention. The first concerns their level of subsistence, long deemed to have been one of chronic scarcity and want. According to the still controversial findings of the anthropologist Marshall Sahlins, this notion of scarcity is not true. His studies of several preliterate peoples found that they could easily increase their provisioning if they so desired. The condition usually perceived by contemporary observers as scarcity is felt by preliterate peoples as satiety; Sahlins describes preliterate life as the first "affluent society."

A second discernible characteristic of preliterate economic systems is the difficulty of describing any part of their activities as constituting an "economy." No special modes of coordination distinguish the activities of hunting or gathering or the procedures of distribution from the rest of social life, so there is nothing in Eskimo or Kalahari or Bedouin life that requires a special vocabulary or conceptual apparatus called "economics." The economy as a network of provisioning activities is completely absorbed within and fully inextricable from the traditional mode of existence as a whole.

CENTRALIZED STATES

Very little is known of the origin of the second of the great systems of social coordination—namely, the creation of a central apparatus of command and rulership. From ancient clusters of population, impressive civilizations emerged in Egypt, China, and India during the 3rd millennium BCE, bringing with them not only dazzling advances in culture but also the potent instrument of state power as a new moving force in history.

The appearance of these centralized states is arguably the single most decisive alteration in economic, and perhaps in all, history. Although tradition still exerted its stabilizing and preserving role at the base of these societies—Adam Smith said that in "Indostan or ancient Egypt…every man was bound by a principle of religion to follow the occupation of his father"—the vast temple complexes, irrigation systems, fortifications, and cities of ancient India and China and of the kingdoms of the Inca and Maya attest unmistakably to the difference that the organizing principle of command brought to economic life. It lay in the ability of centralized authority to wrest considerable portions of the population away from their traditional occupations and to use their labour energies in ways that expressed the wishes of a ruling personage or small elite.

Herodotus recounts how the pharaoh Khufu used his power to this end:

[He] ordered all Egyptians to work for himself. Some, accordingly, were appointed to draw stones from the quarries in the Arabian mountains down to the Nile, others he ordered to receive the stones when transported in vessels across the river....And they worked to the number of a hundred thousand men at a time, each party during three months. The time during which the people were thus harassed by toil lasted ten years on the road which they constructed, and along which they drew the stones; a work, in my opinion, not much less than the Pyramids.

The creation of these monuments illustrates an important general characteristic of all systems of command. Such systems, unlike those based on tradition, can generate immense surpluses of wealth—indeed, the very purpose of a command organization of economic life can be said to lie in securing such a surplus. Command systems thereby acquire the wherewithal to change the conditions of material existence in far-reaching ways. Prior to the modern era, when command became the main coordination system for socialism, it was typical of such command systems to use this productive power principally to cater to the consumption or to the power and glory of their ruling elites.

Moral judgments aside, this highly personal disposition of surplus has the further consequence of again resisting any sharp analytic distinction between the workings of the economy of such a society and that of its larger social framework. The methods of what could be termed "economic coordination" in a command system are identical with those that guide the imperial state in all its historical engagements, just as in primitive society the methods that coordinate the activities of production and distribution are indistinguishable from those that shape family or religious or cultural life. Thus, in command systems, as in tradition-based ones, there is no autonomous economic sphere of life separate from the basic organizing principles of the society in general.

COMMAND ECONOMY

A command economy is an economic system in which the means of production are publicly owned and economic activity is controlled by a central authority that assigns quantitative production goals and allots raw materials to productive enterprises. In such a system, determining the proportion of total product used for investment rather than consumption becomes a centrally made political decision. After this decision has been made, the central planners work out the assortment of goods to be produced and the quotas for each enterprise. Consumers may influence the planners' decisions indirectly if the planners take into consideration the surpluses and shortages that have developed in the market. The only direct choice made by consumers, however, is among the commodities already produced.

Prices are also set by the central planners, but they do not serve, as in a market economy, as signals to producers of goods to increase or decrease production. Instead, they are used mainly as instruments of the central planners in their efforts to reconcile the total demand for consumer goods with the supply available, allowing also for revenues to the state.

The central authority in a command economy assigns production goals in terms of physical units and allocates physical quantities of raw materials to enterprises. The process for a large economy with millions of products is extremely complex and has encountered a number of difficulties in practice.

Central planning of this kind is not without apparent advantages, however, since it enables a government to mobilize resources quickly on a national scale during wartime or some other national emergency. But the costs of centralized policies are real and quite high. Moreover, it is often the case that much of the burden of these costs is shifted away from the government. One example is the military draft, which largely shifts the cost of mobilizing troops from the government to the draftees, who could be employed at a higher rate of pay elsewhere.

PRECONDITIONS FOR MARKET SOCIETY

These general considerations throw into relief the nature of the economic problems that must be resolved in a system of market coordination. Such a system must be distinguished from the mere existence of marketplaces, which originated far back in history. Trading relations between the ancient Levantine kingdoms and the pharaohs of Egypt about 1400 BC are known from the tablets of Tell el-Amarna. A thousand years later Isocrates boasted of the thriving trade of Classical Greece, while a rich and varied network of commodity exchange and an established market for monetary capital were prominent features of Classical Rome.

These flourishing institutions of commerce testify to the ancient lineages of money, profit-mindedness, and mercantile groups, but they do not testify to the presence of a market system. In premarket societies, markets were the means to join suppliers and demanders of luxuries and superfluities, but they were not the means by which the provision of essential goods and services was assured. For these purposes, ancient kingdoms or republics still looked to tradition and command, utilizing slavery as a basic source of labour (including captives taken in war) and viewing with disdain the profit orientation of market life. This disdain

This lithograph shows the marketplace in Corinth, an ancient Greek city-state between Athens and Sparta.

applied particularly to the use of the incentives and penalties of the market as a means of marshaling labour. Aristotle expressed the common feeling of his age when he declared, "The condition of the free man is that he does not live for the benefit of another." With the exception of some military service, nonslave labour was simply not for sale.

The difference between a society with flourishing markets and a market-coordinated society is not, therefore, merely one of attitudes. Before a system orchestrated by the market can replace one built on obedience to communal or authoritarian pressure, the social orders dependent on tradition and command must be replaced by a new order in which individuals are expected to fend for themselves and in which all are permitted—even encouraged—to improve their material condition. Individuals cannot have such aims, much less such "rights," until the dominant authority of custom or hierarchical privilege has been swept away. A rearrangement of this magnitude entails wrenching dislocations of power and prerogative. A market society is not, consequently, merely a society coordinated by markets. It is, of necessity, a social order with a distinctive structure of laws and privileges.

It follows that a market society requires an organizing principle that, by definition, can no longer be the respect accorded to tradition or the obedience owed to a political elite. This principle becomes the generalized search for material gain—a striving for betterment that is unique to each individual. Such a condition of universal upward striving is unimaginable in a traditional society and could be seen only as a dangerous threat in a society built on established hierarchies of authority. But, for reasons that will be seen, it is accommodated by, and indeed constitutive of, the workings of a market system.

The process by which these institutional and attitudinal changes are brought about constitutes a grand theme—perhaps the grand theme—of economic history from roughly the 5th to the 18th and even into the 19th century in Europe. In terms of political history, the period was marked by the collapse of the Roman Empire, the rise of feudalism, and the slow formation of national states. In social terms, it featured the end of an order characterized by an imperial retinue at the top and massive slavery at the bottom, that order's replacement by gradations of feudal vassalage descending from lord to serf, and the eventual appearance of a bourgeois society with distinct classes of workers, landlords, and entrepreneurs. From the economist's perspective, the period was marked by the breakdown of a coordinative mechanism of centralized command, the rise of the mixed pressures of tradition and local command characteristic of the feudal manor, and the gradual displacement of those pressures by the material penalties and rewards of an all-embracing market network. In this vast transformation the rise of the market mechanism became crucial as the means by which the new social formation of capitalism ensured its self-provisioning, but the mechanism itself rested on deeper-lying social, cultural, and political changes that created the capitalist order it served.

A lord oversees serfs planting vine grapes in medieval Italy.

To attempt to trace these lineages of capitalism would take one far beyond the confines of the present subject. Suffice it to remark that the emergence of the new order was first given expression in the 10th and 11th centuries, when a rising mercantile "estate" began to bargain successfully for recognition and protection with the local lords and monarchs of the early Middle Ages. Not until the 16th and 17th centuries was there a "commercialization" of the aristocratic strata, many of whose members fared poorly in an ever more money-oriented world and accordingly contracted marriages with wealthy merchant families (whom they would not have received at home a generation or two earlier) to preserve their social and material status. Of greatest significance, however, was the transformation of the lower orders, a process that began in Elizabethan England but did not take place en masse until the 18th and even the 19th century. As feudal lords became profit-minded landlords, peasants moved off the land to become an agricultural proletariat in search of the best wages obtainable, because traditional subsistence was no longer available. Thus, the market network extended its disciplinary power over "free" labour—the resource that had previously eluded its influence. The resulting social order made it possible for markets to coordinate production and distribution in a manner never before possible.

FROM MERCANTILISM TO COMMERCIAL CAPITALISM

It is usual to describe the earliest stages of capitalism as mercantilism, the word denoting the central importance of the merchant overseas traders who rose to prominence in 17th- and 18th-century England, Germany, and the Low Countries. In numerous pamphlets, these merchants defended the principle that their trading activities buttressed the interest of the sovereign power, even when, to the consternation of the court, this required sending "treasure" (bullion) abroad. As the pamphleteers explained, treasure used in this way became itself a commodity in foreign trade, in which, as the 17th-century merchant Thomas Mun wrote, "we must ever observe this rule; to sell more to strangers than we consume of theirs in value."

For all its trading mentality, mercantilism was only partially a market-coordinated system. Adam Smith complained bitterly about the government monopolies that granted exclusive trading rights to groups such as the East India or the Turkey companies, and modern commentators have emphasized the degree to which mercantilist economies relied on regulated, not free, prices and wages. The economic society that Smith described in *The Wealth of Nations* in 1776 is much closer to modern society, although it differs in many respects, as shall be seen. This 18th-century stage is called "commercial capitalism," although it should be noted that the word *capitalism* itself does not actually appear in the pages of Smith's book.

Smith's society is nonetheless recognizable as capitalist precisely because of the prominence of those elements that had been absent in its mercantilist form. For example, with few exceptions, the production and distribution of all goods and services were entrusted to market forces rather than to the rules and regulations that had abounded a century earlier. The level of wages was likewise mainly determined by the interplay of the supply of, and the demand for, labour—not by the rulings of local magistrates. A company's earnings were exposed to competition rather than protected by government monopoly.

Perhaps of greater importance in perceiving Smith's world as capitalist as well as market-oriented is its clear division of society into an economic realm and a political realm. The role of government had been gradually narrowed until Smith could describe its duties as consisting of only three functions: (1) the provision of national defense, (2) the protection of each member of society from the injustice or oppression of any other, and (3) the erection and maintenance of those public works and public institutions (including education) that would not repay the expense of any private enterpriser, although they might "do much more than repay it" to society as a whole. And if the role of government in daily life had been delimited, that of commerce had been expanded. The accumulation of capital had come to be recognized as the driving engine of the system. The expansion of "capitals"—Smith's term for firms—was the determining power by which the market system was launched on its historic course.

Thus, *The Wealth of Nations* offered the first precise description of both the dynamics and the coordinative processes of capitalism. The latter were entrusted to the market mechanism—which is to say, to the universal drive for material betterment, curbed and contained by the necessary condition of competition. Smith's great perception was that the combination of this drive and counterforce would direct productive activity toward those goods and services for which the public had the means and desire to pay while forcing producers to satisfy those wants at prices that yielded no more than normal profits. Later economists would devote a great deal of attention to the question of whether competition in fact adequately constrains the workings of the acquisitive drive and whether a market system might not display cycles and crises unmentioned in *The Wealth of Nations*. These were questions unknown to Smith, because the institutions that would produce them, above all the development of large-scale industry, lay in the future. Given these historical realities, one can only admire Smith's perception of the market as a means of solving the economic problem.

Smith also saw that the competitive search for capital accumulation would impart a distinctive tendency to a society that harnessed its motive force. He pointed out that the most obvious way for a manufacturer to gain wealth was to expand his enterprise by hiring additional workers. As firms expanded their individual operations, manufacturers found that they could subdivide complex tasks into simpler ones and could then speed along these simpler tasks by providing their operatives with machinery. Thus, the expansion of firms made possible an ever-finer division of labour, and the finer division of labour, in turn, improved profits by lowering the costs of production and thereby encouraging the further enlargement of the firms. In this way, the incentives of the

Division of Labour

Division of labour is the separation of a work process into a number of tasks, with each task performed by a separate person or group of persons. It is most often applied to systems of mass production and is one of the basic organizing principles of the assembly line. Breaking down work into simple repetitive tasks eliminates unnecessary motion and limits the handling of different tools and parts. The consequent reduction in production time and the ability to replace craftsmen with lower-paid unskilled workers result in lower production costs and a less expensive final product. Contrary to popular belief, however, division of labour does not necessarily lead to a decrease in skills—known as proletarianization—among the working population. The Scottish economist Adam Smith saw this splitting of tasks as a key to economic progress by providing a cheaper and more efficient means of producing goods.

The French scholar Émile Durkheim first used the phrase *division of labour* in a sociological sense in his discussion of social evolution. Rather than viewing division of labour as a consequence of a desire for material abundance, Durkheim stated that specialization arose from changes in social structure caused by an assumed natural increase in the size and density of population and a corresponding increase in competition for survival. Division of labour functioned to keep societies from breaking apart under these conditions.

The intensive specialization in industrial societies—the refinement and simplification of tasks (especially associated with a machine technology) so that a worker often produces only a small part of a particular commodity—is not usually found in nonindustrialized societies. There is rarely a division of labour within an industry in nonliterate communities, except perhaps for the production of larger goods (such as houses or canoes); in these cases the division is often a temporary one, and each worker is competent to perform other phases of the task. There may be some specialization in types of products (e.g., one worker may produce pottery for religious uses; another, pottery for ordinary uses), but each worker usually performs all steps of the process.

A division of labour based on sex appears to be universal, but the form that this takes varies widely across cultures. Divisions on the basis of age, clan affiliation, hereditary position, or guild membership, as well as regional and craft specialization, are also found.

market system gave rise to the augmentation of the wealth of the nation itself, endowing market society with its all-important historical momentum and at the same time making room for the upward striving of its members.

One final attribute of the emerging system must be noted. This is the tearing apart of the formerly seamless tapestry of social coordination. Under capitalism two realms of authority existed where there had formerly been only one—a realm of political governance for such purposes as war or law and order and a realm of economic governance over the processes of production and distribution. Each realm was largely shielded from the reach of the other. The capitalists who dominated the market system were not automatically entitled to governing power, and the members of government were not entrusted with decisions as to what goods should be produced or how social rewards should be distributed.

This new dual structure brought with it two consequences of immense importance. The first was a limitation of political power that proved of very great importance in establishing democratic forms of government. The second, closer to the present theme, was the need for a new kind of analysis intended to clarify the workings of this new semi-independent realm within the larger social order. As a result, the emergence of capitalism gave rise to the discipline of economics.

FROM COMMERCIAL TO INDUSTRIAL CAPITALISM

Commercial capitalism proved to be only transitional. The succeeding form would be distinguished by the pervasive mechanization and industrialization of its productive processes, changes that introduced new dynamic tendencies into the economic system while significantly transforming the social and physical landscape.

The transformative agency was already present in Smith's day, observable in a few coal mines where steam-driven engines invented by Thomas Newcomen pumped water out of the pits. The diffusion and penetration of such machinery-driven processes of production during the first quarter of the 19th century has been traditionally called "the" Industrial Revolution, although historians today stress the long germination of the revolution and the many phases through which it passed. There is no doubt, however, that a remarkable confluence of advances in agriculture, cotton spinning and weaving, iron manufacture, and machine-tool design and the harnessing of mechanical power began to alter the character of capitalism profoundly in the last years of the 18th century and the first decades of the 19th.

The alterations did not affect the driving motive of the system or its reliance on market forces as its coordinative principles. Their effect was rather on the cultural complexion of the society that contained these

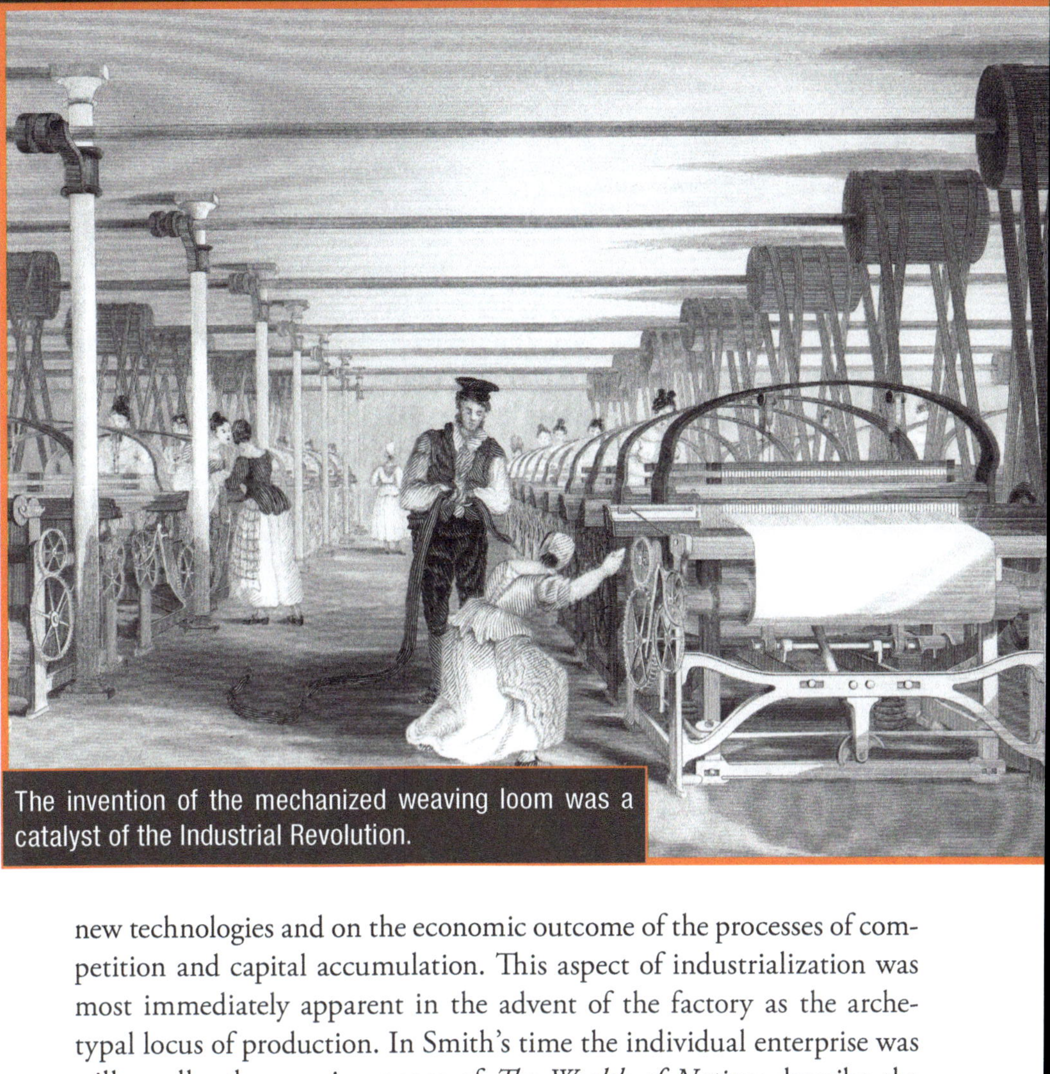

The invention of the mechanized weaving loom was a catalyst of the Industrial Revolution.

new technologies and on the economic outcome of the processes of competition and capital accumulation. This aspect of industrialization was most immediately apparent in the advent of the factory as the archetypal locus of production. In Smith's time the individual enterprise was still small—the opening pages of *The Wealth of Nations* describe the effects of the division of labour in a 10-man pin factory—but by the early 19th century the increasing mechanization of labour, coupled with the application of waterpower and steam power, had raised the size of the workforce in an ordinary textile mill to several hundreds; by mid-century in the steel mills it was up to several thousands, and by the end of the century in the railways it was in the tens of thousands.

The increase in the scale of employment brought a marked change in the character of work itself. In Smith's day the social distance between employer and labourer was still sufficiently small that the very word *manufacturer* implied an occupation (a mechanic) as well as an ownership position. However, early in the 19th century William Blake referred to factories as "dark Satanic mills" in his epic poem *Jerusalem*, and by the 1830s a great gulf had opened between the manufacturers, who were now a propertied business class, and the men, women, and children who tended machinery and laboured in factories for 10- and 12-hour stints. It was from the spectacle of mill labour, described in unsparing detail by the inspectors authorized by the first Factory Act of 1802, that Marx drew much of the indignation that animated his analysis of capitalism. More important, it was from this same factory setting, and from the urban squalor that industrialization also brought, that capitalism derived much of the social consciousness—sometimes revolutionary, sometimes reformist—that was to play so large a part in its subsequent political life. Works such as Charles Dickens's *Hard Times* (1854) depicted the factory system's inhumanity and the underlying economic doctrines that supposedly justified it. While these works brought attention to the social problems stemming from industrialization, they also tended to discount the significant improvements in the overall standard of living (as measured by the increases in life expectancy and material comforts) that accompanied modernization. Country life of just a generation earlier had been no less cruel, and in some respects it was more inhuman than the factory system being criticized. Those critics who failed to compare the era of industrialization with the one that immediately preceded it also failed to account for the social and economic progress that had touched the lives of ordinary people.

The degradation of the physical and social landscape was the aspect of industrialization that first attracted attention, but it was its slower-acting impact on economic growth that was ultimately to be judged its most significant effect. A single statistic may dramatize this process. Between 1788 and 1839 the output of pig iron in Britain rose from

68,000 to 1,347,000 tons. To fully grasp the significance of this 20-fold increase, one has to consider the proliferation of iron pumps, iron machine tools, iron pipes, iron rails, and iron beams that it made possible; these iron implements, in turn, contributed to faster and more dependable production systems. This was the means by which the first Industrial Revolution promoted economic growth, not immediately but with gathering momentum. Thirty years later this effect would be repeated with even more spectacular results when the Bessemer converter ushered in the age of steel rails, ships, machines, girders, wires, pipes, and containers.

The most important consequence of the industrialization of capitalism was therefore its powerful effect on enhancing what Marx called "the forces of production"—the source of what is now called the standard of living. The Swiss economic demographer Paul Bairoch calculated that gross national product (GNP) per capita in the developed countries rose from $180 in the 1750s (in dollars of 1960 purchasing power) to $780 in the 1930s and then to $3,000 in the 1980s, whereas the per capita income of the less-developed countries remained unchanged at about $180–$190 from 1750 to 1930 and thereafter rose only to $410 in 1980. (This seemingly persistent gap between the richest and the poorest countries, which contradicts the predictions of the standard theory of economic growth, has increasingly occupied the attention of contemporary economists. Although the question is answered in part by explaining that the rich countries have experienced industrialization and the poor ones have not, the question remains why some have experienced industrialization and others have not.)

The development of industrialization was accompanied by periodic instability in the 18th and 19th centuries. Not surprisingly, then, one side effect of industrialization was the effort to minimize or prevent economic shocks by linking firms together into cartels or trusts or simply into giant integrated enterprises. Although these efforts dampened the repercussions of individual miscalculations, they were insufficient to guard against the effects of speculative panics or commercial convulsions. By the end of the 19th century, economic depressions had become a worrisome and recurrent problem, and the Great Depression of the 1930s rocked the entire capitalist world. During that debacle, GNP in the United States fell by almost 50 percent, business investment fell by 94 percent, and unemployment rose from 3.2 to nearly 25 percent of the civilian labour force. Economists have long debated the causes of the extraordinary increase in economic instability from 1830 to 1930. Some point to the impact of growth in the scale of production evidenced by the shift from small pin factories to giant enterprises. Others emphasize the role of miscalculations and mismatches in production. And still other explanations range from the inherent instability of capitalist production (particularly for large-scale enterprises) to the failure of government policy (especially with regard to the monetary system).

FROM INDUSTRIAL TO STATE CAPITALISM

The perceived problem of inherent instability takes on further importance insofar as it is a principal cause of the next structural phase of the system. The new phase is often described as state capitalism because its outstanding feature is the enlargement in size and functions of the public realm. In 1929, for example, total U.S. government expenditures—federal, state, and local—came to less than one-tenth of GNP; from the 1970s they amounted to roughly one-third. This increase is observable in all major capitalist nations, many of which have reached considerably higher ratios of government disbursements to GNP than the United States.

At the same time, the function of government changed as decisively as its size. Already by the last quarter of the 19th century, the emergence of great industrial trusts had provoked legislation in the United States (although not in Europe) to curb the monopolistic tendencies of industrialization. Apart from these antitrust laws and the regulation of a few industries of special public concern, however, the functions of the federal government were not significantly broadened from Smith's vision. Prior to the Great Depression, for example, the great bulk of federal outlays went for defense and international relations, for general administrative expense and interest on the debt, and for the post office.

The Great Depression radically altered this limited view of government in the United States, as it had earlier begun to widen it in Europe. The provision of old-age pensions, relief for the hungry and poor, and a dole for the unemployed were all policies inaugurated by the administration of Pres. Franklin D. Roosevelt, following the example of similar enlargements of government functions in Britain, France, and Germany. From the 1970s onward, such new kinds of federal spending—under the designation of social security, health, education, and welfare programs—grew to be 20 to 50 percent larger than the traditional categories of federal spending.

Thus, one very important element in the advent of a new stage of capitalism was the emergence of a large public sector expected to serve as a guarantor of public economic well-being, a function that would never have occurred to Smith. A second and equally important departure was the new assumption that governments themselves were responsible for the general course of economic conditions. This was a change of policy orientation that also emerged from the challenge of the Great Depression. Once regarded as a matter beyond remedy, the general level of national income came to be seen by the end of the 1930s as the responsibility of government, although the measures taken to improve conditions were on the whole timid, often wrongheaded (such as highly protectionist trade policies), and only modestly successful. Nonetheless, the appearance in that decade of a new economic accountability for government constitutes in itself sufficient reason to describe capitalism today in terms that distinguish it from its industrial, but largely unguided, past.

There is little doubt that capitalism will continue to undergo still further structural alterations. Technological advances are rapidly reducing to near insignificance the once-formidable barriers and opportunities of economic geography. Among the startling consequences of this technological leveling of the world have been the large displacements of high-tech manufacturing from Europe and North America to the low-wage regions of Southwest Asia, Latin America, and Africa. Another change has been the unprecedented growth of international finance to the point that, by the beginning of the 21st century, the total value of transactions in foreign exchange was estimated to be at least 20 times that of all foreign movements of goods and services. This boundary-blind internationalization of finance, combined with the boundary-defying ability of large corporations to locate their operations in low-wage countries, poses a challenge to the traditional economic sovereignty of nations, a challenge arising from the new capabilities of capital itself.

A third change again involves the international economy, this time through the creation of new institutions for the management of

Though designed in the United States, Apple products are produced in other countries, such as China.

international economic trade. A number of capitalist nations have met the challenges of the fast-growing international economy by joining the energies of the private sector (including organized labour) to the financial and negotiating powers of the state. This "corporatist" approach, most clearly evident in the organization of the Japanese economy, was viewed with great promise in the 1980s but in the 1990s was found to be severely vulnerable to opportunistic behaviour by individuals in both the public and the private sectors. Thus, at the onset of the 21st century, the consensus on the economic role of government in capitalism shifted back from the social democratic interventionism of the Keynesian system and the managed market economies of the "Asian tigers" (countries such as Hong Kong, Singapore, Malaysia, and South Korea that experienced rapid growth in the late 20th century) to the more noninterventionist model of Adam Smith and the classical economists.

It is not necessary, however, to venture risky predictions concerning economic policy. Rather, it seems more useful to posit two generalizations. The first emphasizes that capitalism in all its variations continues to be distinguished from other economic systems by the priority accorded to the drive for wealth and the centrality of the competitive mechanism that channels this drive toward those ends that the market rewards. The spirit of enterprise, fueled by the acquisitive culture of the market, is the source of the dynamism of capitalism. The second generalization is that this driving force and constraining mechanism appear to be compatible with a wide variety of institutional settings, including substantial variations in the relationships between the private and public sectors. The form of capitalism taken also differs between nations, because the practice of it is embedded within cultures; even the forces of globalization and the threat of homogenization have proved to be more myth than reality. Markets cater to national culture as much as national culture mutates to conform to the discipline of profit and loss. It is to this very adaptability that capitalism appears to owe its continued vitality.

CHAPTER SIX

CRITICISMS OF CAPITALISM AND CENTRALLY PLANNED SYSTEMS

Advocates and critics of capitalism agree that its distinctive contribution to history has been the encouragement of economic growth. Capitalist growth is not, however, regarded as an unalloyed benefit by its critics. Its negative side derives from three dysfunctions that reflect its market origins.

THE UNRELIABILITY OF GROWTH

The first of these problems is already familiar from the previous discussion of the stages of capitalist development. Many critics have alleged that the capitalist system suffers from inherent instability that has characterized and plagued the system since the advent of industrialization. Because capitalist growth is driven by profit expectations, it fluctuates with the changes in technological or social opportunities for capital accumulation. As opportunities appear, capital rushes in to take advantage of them, bringing as a consequence the familiar attributes of a boom. Sooner or later, however, the rush subsides as the demand for the new products or services becomes saturated, bringing a halt to investment, a shakeout in the main industries caught up in the previous boom, and the advent of recession. Hence, economic growth comes at the price of a succession of market gluts as booms meet their inevitable end.

This criticism did not receive its full exposition until the publication of the first volume of Marx's *Das Kapital* in 1867. For Marx, the path of growth is not only unstable for the reasons just mentioned—Marx called such uncoordinated movements the "anarchy" of the market—but increasingly unstable. Marx believed that the reason for this is also familiar. It is the result of the industrialization process, which leads toward large-scale enterprises. As each saturation brings growth to a halt, a process of winnowing takes place in which the more successful firms are able to acquire the assets of the less successful. Thus, the very dynamics of growth tend to concentrate capital into ever-larger firms. This leads to still more massive disruptions when the next boom ends, a process that terminates, according to Marx, only when the temper of the working class snaps and capitalism is replaced by socialism.

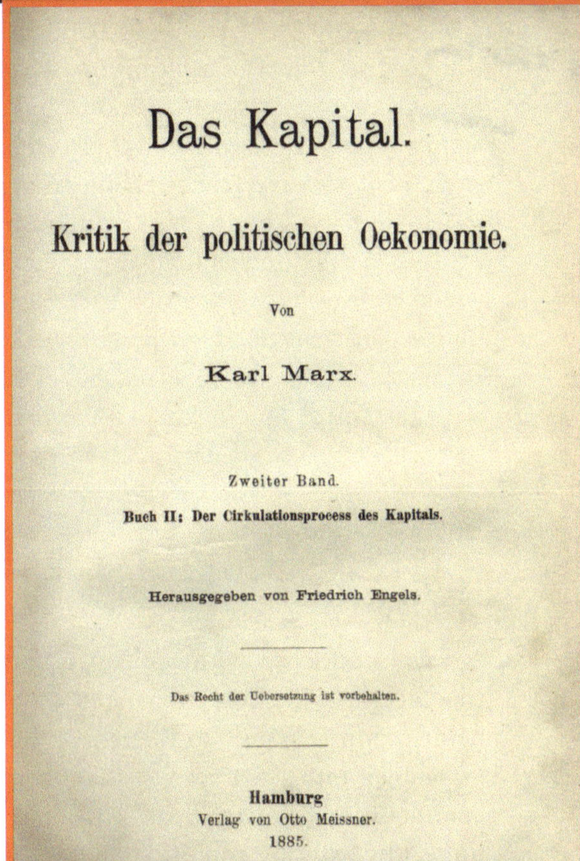

Das Kapital.

Kritik der politischen Oekonomie.

Von

Karl Marx.

Zweiter Band.

Buch II: Der Cirkulationsprocess des Kapitals.

Herausgegeben von Friedrich Engels.

Das Recht der Uebersetzung ist vorbehalten.

Hamburg
Verlag von Otto Meissner.
1885.

In *Das Kapital*, Marx posits that capitalism is based on exploitation of labour.

Beginning in the 1930s, Marx's apocalyptic expectations were largely replaced by the less-violent but equally disquieting views of the English economist John Maynard Keynes, first set forth in his influential

The General Theory of Employment, Interest, and Money (1936). Keynes believed that the basic problem of capitalism is not so much its vulnerability to periodic saturations of investment as its likely failure to recover from them. He raised the possibility that a capitalist system could remain indefinitely in a condition of equilibrium despite high unemployment, a possibility not only entirely novel (even Marx believed that the system would recover its momentum after each crisis) but also made plausible by the persistent unemployment of the 1930s. Keynes therefore raised the prospect that growth would end in stagnation, a condition for which the only remedy he saw was "a somewhat comprehensive socialization of investment."

THE QUALITY OF GROWTH

A second criticism with respect to market-driven growth focuses on the adverse side effects generated by a system of production that is held accountable only to the test of profitability. It is in the nature of a complex industrial society that the production processes of many commodities generate "bads" as well as "goods"—e.g., toxic wastes or unhealthy working conditions as well as useful products.

The catalog of such market-generated ills is very long. Smith himself warned that the division of labour, by routinizing work, would render workers "as stupid and ignorant as it is possible for a human creature to become," and Marx raised the spectre of alienation as the social price paid for subordinating production to the imperatives of profit making. Other economists warned that the introduction of technology designed to cut labour costs would create permanent unemployment. In modern times much attention has focused on the power of physical and chemical processes to surpass the carrying capacity of the environment—a concern made cogent by various types of environmental damage arising from excessive discharges of industrial effluents and pollutants. Because these social and ecological challenges spring from the extraordinary powers of technology, they can be viewed as side effects of socialist as well as capitalist growth. But the argument can be made that market growth, by virtue of its overriding obedience to profit, is congenitally blind to such externalities.

EQUITY

A third criticism of capitalist growth concerns the fairness with which capitalism distributes its expanding wealth or with which it shares its recurrent hardships. This criticism assumes both specific and general forms.

The specific form focuses on disparities in income among layers of the population. At the turn of the 21st century in the United States, for example, the lowest fifth of all households received only 3.6 percent of total income, whereas the topmost fifth received 49 percent. Significantly, this disparity results from the concentration of assets in the upper brackets. Also, the disparity is the consequence of highly skewed patterns of corporate rewards that typically give, say, chief executive officers of large companies 50 to 100 times more income than those of ordinary office or factory employees. Income disparities, however, should be understood in perspective, as they stem from a number of causes. In its 1995 annual report the Federal Reserve Bank of Dallas observed:

> **By definition, there will always be a bottom 20 percent, but only in a strict caste society will it contain the same individuals and families year after year.**

Moving from specific examples of distribution to a more general level, the criticism may be broadened to an indictment of the market principle itself as the regulator of incomes. An advocate of market-determined distribution will declare that in a market-based society, with certain exceptions, people tend to be paid what they are worth—that

Distribution of Wealth and Income

The distribution of wealth and income is the way in which the wealth and income of a nation are divided among its population, or the way in which the wealth and income of the world are divided among nations. Such patterns of distribution are discerned and studied by various statistical means, all of which are based on data of varying degrees of reliability.

Wealth is an accumulated store of possessions and financial claims. It may be given a monetary value if prices can be determined for each of the possessions; this process can be difficult when the possessions are such that they are not likely to be offered for sale. Income is a net total of the flow of payments received in a given time period. Some countries collect statistics on wealth from legally required evaluations of the estates of deceased persons, which may or may not be indicative of what is possessed by the living. In many countries, annual tax statements that measure income provide more or less reliable information. Differences in definitions of income—whether, for example, income should include payments that are transfers rather than the result of productive activity, or capital gains or losses that change the value of an individual's wealth—make comparisons difficult.

In order to classify patterns of national wealth and income, a basis of classification must be determined. One classification system categorizes wealth and income on the basis of the ownership of factors of production: labour, land, capital, and, occasionally, entrepreneurship, whose respective forms of income are labeled wages, rent, interest, and profit. Personal distribution statistics, usually developed from tax reports, categorize wealth and income on a per capita basis.

Gross national income (GNI) per capita provides a rough measure of annual national income per person in different countries. Countries that have a sizable modern industrial sector have a much higher GNI per capita than countries that are less developed. In the early 21st century, for example, the World Bank estimated that the per-capita GNI was approximately $10,000 and above for the most-developed countries but was less than $825 for the least-developed countries. Income also varies greatly within countries. In a high-income country such as the United States, there is considerable variation among industries, regions, rural and urban areas, females and males, and ethnic groups. While the bulk of the U.S. population has a middle income that is derived largely from earnings, wages vary considerably depending on occupation.

A significant proportion of an economy's higher incomes will derive from investment rather than earnings. It is often the case that the higher the income, the higher the investment-derived portion tends to be. Because most fortunes require long periods to accumulate, the existence of a class of very wealthy persons can result from the ability of those persons to retain their fortunes and pass them on to descendants. Earned incomes are influenced by a different kind of inheritance. Access to well-paid jobs and social status is largely the product of education and opportunity. Typically, therefore, well-educated children of wealthier parents tend to retain their parents' status and earning power. A dynamic economy, however, increases the likelihood of attaining wealth and status through individual effort alone.

is, their incomes will reflect the value of their contribution to production. Thus, market-based rewards lead to the efficiency of the productive system and thereby maximize the total income available for distribution. This argument is countered at two levels. Marxist critics contend that labourers in a capitalist economy are systematically paid less than the value of their work by virtue of the superior bargaining power of employers, so that the claim of efficiency masks an underlying condition of exploitation. Other critics question the criterion of efficiency itself, which counts every dollar of input and output but pays no heed to the moral or social or aesthetic qualities of either and which excludes workers from expressing their own preferences as to the most appropriate decisions for their firms.

CORRECTIVE MEASURES

Various measures have been taken by capitalist societies to meet these criticisms, although it must be recognized that a deep disagreement divides economists with respect to the accuracy of the criticisms, let alone the appropriate corrective measures to be adopted if these criticisms are valid. A substantial body of economists believe that many of the difficulties of the system spring not from its own workings but from well-meaning attempts to block or channel them. Thus, with respect to the problem of instability, supporters of the market system believe that capitalism, left alone as much as possible, will naturally corroborate the trend of economic expansion that has marked its history. They also expect that whatever instabilities appear tend quickly to correct themselves, provided that government plays a generally passive role. Market-oriented economists do not deny that the system can give rise to qualitative or distributional ills, but they tend to believe that these are more than compensated for by its general expansive properties. Where specific problems remain, such as damage to the environment or serious poverty, the prescription often seeks to utilize the market system itself as the corrective agency—e.g., alleviating poverty through negative income taxes rather than with welfare payments or controlling pollution by charging fees on the outflow of wastes rather than by banning the discharge of pollutants.

Opposing this view is a much more interventionist approach rooted in generally Keynesian and welfare-oriented policies. This view doubts the intrinsic momentum or reliability of capitalist growth and is therefore prepared to use active government means, both fiscal and monetary, to combat recession. It is also more skeptical of the likelihood of improving the quality or the equity of society by market means and, although not opposing these, looks more favourably on direct regulatory intervention and on specific programs of assistance to disprivileged groups.

Despite this philosophical division of opinion, a fair degree of practical consensus was reached on a number of issues in the 1950s and '60s. Although there are differences in policy style and determination from one nation to the next, all capitalist governments have taken measures to overcome recession—whether by lowering taxes, by borrowing and spending, or by easing interest rates—and all pursue the opposite kinds of policies in inflationary times. It cannot be said that these policies have been unqualified successes, either in bringing about vigorous or steady growth or in ridding the system of its inflationary tendencies. Yet, imperfect though they are, these measures seem to have been sufficient to prevent the development of socially destructive depressions on the order of the Great Depression of the 1930s. It is not the eradication but the limitation of instability that has been a signal achievement of all advanced capitalist countries since World War II. It should be noted, however, that these remedial measures have little or no international application. Although the World Bank and the International Monetary Fund make efforts on behalf of developing countries, no institution exists to control credit for the world (as do the central banks that control it for individual nations); no global spending or taxing authority can speed up, or hold back, the pace of production for industrial regions as a whole; no agency effectively oversees the availability of credit for the

Headquartered in Washington, D.C., the World Bank is the largest source of financial aid to developing nations.

developing nations or the feasibility of the terms on which it may be extended. Thus, some critics of globalization contend that the internationalization of capitalism may exert destabilizing influences for which no policy corrective as yet exists.

A broadly similar appraisal can be made with respect to the redress of specific threats that emerge as unintended consequences of the market system. The issue is largely one of scale. Specific problems can often be redressed by market incentives to alter behaviour (paying a fee for returning used bottles) or, when the effect is more serious, by outright prohibition (bans on child labour or on dangerous chemical fertilizers). The problem becomes less amenable to control, however, when the market generates unintended consequences of large proportions, such as traffic congestion in cities. The difficulty here is that the correction of such externalities requires the support and cooperation of the public and thereby crosses the line from the economic into the political arena, often making redress more difficult to obtain. On a still larger scale, the remedy for some problems may require international agreements, and these often raise conflicts of interest between the nation generating the ill effects as a by-product of its own production and those suffering from the effects. The problem of acid rain originating in one country but falling in another is a case in point. Again the economic problem becomes political and its control more complicated.

A number of remedies have been applied to the distributional problems of capitalism. No advanced capitalist country today allows the market to distribute income without supplementing or altering the resulting pattern of rewards through taxes, subsidies, welfare systems, or entitlement payments such as old-age pensions and health benefits. In the United States, these transfer payments, as they are called, amount to some 10 percent of total consumer income; in a number of European nations, they come to considerably more. The result has been to lessen considerably the incidence of officially measured poverty.

Yet these examples of successful corrective action by governments do not go unchallenged by economists who are concerned that some of the "cures" applied to social problems may be worse than the "disease." While admitting that the market system fails to live up to its ideal, these economists argue that government correctives and collective decision making must be subjected to the same critical scrutiny leveled against the market system. Markets may fail, in other words, but so might governments. The stagflation of the 1970s, the fiscal crises of some democratic states in the 1980s, and the double-digit unemployment in western Europe in the 1990s set the stage for the 21st century by raising serious doubts about the ability of government correctives to solve market problems.

CENTRALLY PLANNED SYSTEMS

No survey of comparative economic systems would be complete without an account of centrally planned systems, the modern descendants of the command economies of the imperial past. In sharpest possible contrast to those earlier tributary arrangements, however, modern command societies have virtually all been organized in the name of socialism—that is, with the function of command officially administered on behalf of an ideology purported to serve the broad masses of the population.

Socialist central planning needs to be differentiated from the idea of socialism itself. The latter draws on moral precepts of concern for the needy that can be discovered in the Judeo-Christian tradition and derives its general social orientation from Gerrard Winstanley's Diggers movement during the English Civil Wars in the mid-17th century: "The Earth," Winstanley wrote, "was made by Almighty God to be a Common Treasury of livelihood to the whole of mankind...without respect of persons."

Socialism as a means of orchestrating a modern industrial system did not receive explicit attention until the Russian Revolution in 1917. In his pamphlet *The State and Revolution*, written before he came to power, Vladimir Lenin envisaged the task of coordinating a socialist economy as little more than delivering production to central collecting points from which it would be distributed according to need—an operation requiring no more than "the extraordinarily simple operations of watching, recording, and issuing receipts, within the reach of anybody who can read and who knows the first four rules of arithmetic." After the revolution it soon became apparent that the problem was a great deal more difficult than that. The mobilization of human capital required the complex determination of appropriate amounts and levels of pay, and the transportation of foodstuffs from the countryside posed the awkward question of the degree to which the "bourgeois" peasantry would have to be accommodated. As civil war raged in the country, these problems intensified until production fell to a catastrophic 14 percent of prewar levels. By the end of 1920, the economic system of the Soviet Union was on the verge of collapse.

To forestall disaster, Lenin instituted the New Economic Policy (NEP), which amounted to a partial restoration of capitalism, especially in retail trade, small-scale production, and agriculture. Only the "commanding heights" of the economy remained in government hands. The NEP resuscitated the economy but opened a period of intense debate

Lenin addressing the Second All-Russian Congress of Soviets in Petrograd (now St. Petersburg) in 1917.

NEW ECONOMIC POLICY (NEP)

The New Economic Policy was the economic policy of the government of the Soviet Union from 1921 to 1928, representing a temporary retreat from its previous policy of extreme centralization and doctrinaire socialism. The policy of War Communism, in effect since 1918, had by 1921 brought the national economy to the point of total breakdown. The Kronshtadt Rebellion of March 1921 convinced the Communist Party and its leader, Vladimir Lenin, of the need to retreat from socialist policies in order to maintain the party's hold on power. Accordingly, the 10th Party Congress in March 1921 introduced the measures of the New Economic Policy. These measures included the return of most agriculture, retail trade, and small-scale light industry to private ownership and management while the state retained control of heavy industry, transport, banking, and foreign trade. Money was reintroduced into the economy in 1922 (it had been abolished under War Communism). The peasantry were allowed to own and cultivate their own land, while paying taxes to the state. The New Economic Policy reintroduced a measure of stability to the economy and allowed the Soviet people to recover from years of war, civil war, and governmental mismanagement. The small businessmen and managers who flourished in this period became known as NEP men.

But the NEP was viewed by the Soviet government as merely a temporary expedient to allow the economy to recover while the Communists solidified their hold on power. By 1925 Nikolay Bukharin had become the foremost supporter of the NEP, while Leon Trotsky was opposed to it and Joseph Stalin was noncommittal. The NEP was dogged by the government's chronic inability to procure enough grain supplies from the peasantry to feed its urban work force. In 1928–29 these grain shortages prompted Joseph Stalin, by then the country's paramount leader, to forcibly eliminate the private ownership of farmland and to collectivize agriculture under the state's control, thus ensuring the procurement of adequate food supplies for the cities in the future. This abrupt policy change, which was accompanied by the destruction of several million of the country's most prosperous private farmers, marked the end of the NEP. It was followed by the reimposition of state control over all industry and commerce in the country by 1931.

as to the use of market incentives versus moral suasion or more coercive techniques. The debate, which remained unresolved during Lenin's life, persisted after his death in 1924 during the subsequent struggle for power between Joseph Stalin, Leon Trotsky, and Nikolay Bukharin. Stalin's rise to power brought a rapid collectivization of the economy. The NEP was abandoned. Private agriculture was converted into collective farming with great cruelty and loss of life; all capitalist markets and private enterprises were quickly and ruthlessly eliminated; and the direction of economic life was consigned to a bureaucracy of ministries and planning agencies. By the 1930s a structure of centralized planning had been put into place that was to coordinate the Russian economy for the next half century.

SOVIET PLANNING

At the centre of the official planning system was the Gosplan (*gos* means "committee"), the top economic planning agency of the Soviet state.

Above the Gosplan were the political arms of the Soviet government, while below it were smaller planning agencies for the various Soviet republics. The Gosplan itself was staffed by economists and statisticians charged with drawing up what amounted to a blueprint for national economic activity. This blueprint, usually based on a five- to seven-year period, translated the major objectives determined by political decision (electrification targets, agricultural goals, transportation networks, and the like) into industry-specific requirements (outputs of generators, fertilizers, steel rails). These general requirements were then referred to ministries charged with the management of the industries in question, where the targets were further broken down into specific outputs (quantities, qualities, shapes, and sizes of steel plates, girders, rods, wires, and so forth) and where lower-level goals were fixed, such as budgets for firms, wage rates for different skill levels, or managerial bonuses.

Planning was not, therefore, entirely a one-way process. General objectives were indeed transmitted from the top down, but, as each ministry and factory inspected its obligations, specific obstacles and difficulties were transmitted from the bottom up. The final plan was thus a compromise between the political objectives of the Central Committee of the Communist Party and the nuts-and-bolts considerations of the echelons charged with its execution. This coordinative mechanism worked reasonably well when the larger objectives of the system called for the kind of crash planning often seen in a war economy. The Soviet economy achieved unprecedented rapid progress in its industrialization drive before World War II and in repairing the devastation that followed the war. Moreover, in areas where the political stakes were high, such as space technology, the planning system was able to concentrate skills and resources regardless of cost, which enabled the Soviet Union on more than one occasion to outperform similar undertakings in the West. Yet, charged with the orchestration of a civilian economy in normal peacetime conditions, the system of centralized planning failed seriously.

Because of its failures, a far-reaching reorganization of the system was set into motion in 1985 by Mikhail Gorbachev, under the banner of perestroika ("restructuring"). The extent of the restructuring can be judged by these proposed changes in the coordinative system: (1) the scope and penetration of central planning were to be greatly curtailed and directed instead toward general economic goals, such as rates of growth, consumption or investment targets, or regional development; (2) planning done for factory enterprises was to be taken up by factories themselves, and decisions were to be guided by considerations of profit and loss; (3) factory managers were no longer to be bound by instructions regarding which suppliers to use or where to distribute their products but were to be free to buy from and to sell to whomever they pleased; (4) managers were also to be free to hire and—more important—to fire workers who had been difficult to discharge; and (5) many kinds of small private enterprises were to be encouraged, especially in farming and the retail trades.

This program represented a dramatic retreat from the original idea of central planning. One cannot say, however, that it also represented a decisive turn from socialism to capitalism, for it was not clear to what extent the restructured planning system might embody other essential features of capitalism, such as private ownership of the means of production and the exclusion of political power from the normal operations of economic life. Nor was it known to what extent economic perestroika was to be accompanied by its political counterpart, glasnost ("openness"). Thus, the degree of change in both the economic structure and the underlying political order remained indeterminate.

The record of perestroika over the rest of the 1980s was disappointing. After an initial flush of enthusiasm, the task of abandoning the centralized planning system proved to be far more difficult than anticipated, in part because the magnitude of such a change would have necessitated the creation of a new structure of economic (managerial) power, independent of, and to some extent in continuous tension with, that of political power, much as under capitalism. Also, the operation of the centralized planning system, freed from some of the coercive pressures of the past but not yet infused with the energies of the market, rapidly deteriorated. Despite bumper crops, for example, it was impossible to move potatoes from the fields to retail outlets, so that rations decreased and rumours of acute food shortages raced through Moscow. By the end of the 1980s, the Soviet system was facing an economic breakdown more severe and far-reaching than the worst capitalist crisis of the 1930s. Not surprisingly, the unrest aroused ancient nationalist rivalries and ambitions, threatening the dismemberment of the Soviet economic and political empire.

As the Soviet central government gradually lost control over the economy at the republic and local levels, the system of central planning eroded without adequate free-market mechanisms to replace it. By 1990 the Soviet economy had slid into near paralysis, and this condition foreshadowed the fall from power of the Soviet Communist Party

Food shortages forced the city of Leningrad (now St. Petersburg) to issue rationing coupons in 1990.

and the breakup of the Soviet Union itself into a group of independent republics in 1991.

Attempts to transform socialist systems into market economies began in eastern and central Europe in 1989 and in the former Soviet Union in 1992. Ambitious privatization programs were pursued in Poland, Hungary, Germany, the Czech Republic, and Russia. In many countries this economic transformation was joined by a transition (although with varying degrees of success) to democratic forms of governance.

MIXED ECONOMIES

The socialist turn from planning toward the market provides a fitting initial conclusion to this overview of the typology of economic systems, for it is apparent that the three ideal types—of tradition, command, and market—have never been attained in wholly pure form. Perhaps the most undiluted of these modes in practice has been that of tradition, the great means of orchestration in prestate economic life. But even in tradition a form of command can be seen in the expected obedience of community members to the sanctions of tradition. In the great command systems of the past, as has been seen, tradition supplied important stabilizing functions, and traces of market exchange served to connect these systems to others beyond their borders. The market system as well has never existed in wholly pure form. Market societies have always taken for granted that tradition would provide the foundation of trustworthiness and honesty without which a market-knit society would require an impossible degree of supervision, and no capitalist society has ever existed without a core of public economic undertakings, of which Adam Smith's triad—defense, law and order, and nonprofitable public works—constitutes the irreducible minimum.

Thus, it is not surprising that the Soviet Union's efforts to find a more flexible amalgam of planning and market were anticipated by several decades of cautious experiment in some of the socialist countries of eastern Europe, especially Yugoslavia and Hungary, and by bold departures from central planning in China after 1979. All these economies existed in some degree of flux as their governments sought configurations best suited to their institutional legacies, political ideologies, and cultural traditions. All of them also encountered problems similar in kind, although not in degree, to those of the Soviet Union as they sought to escape the confines of highly centralized economic control. After the Soviet Union abandoned its control over eastern Europe in 1989–90, most of that region's countries began converting their economies into capitalistlike systems.

Something of this mixed system of coordination can also be seen in the less-developed regions of the world. The panorama of these economies represents a panoply of economic systems, with tradition-dominated tribal societies, absolute monarchies, and semifeudal societies side by side with military socialisms and sophisticated but unevenly developed capitalisms.

Urban growth in China has overtaken rural areas, as illustrated by this vegetable field beside new construction in Hefei.

To some extent, this spectrum reflects the legacy of 19th-century imperialist capitalism, against whose cultural as well as economic hegemony all latecomers have had to struggle. Little can be ventured as to the outcome of this astonishing variety of economic structures. A few may follow the corporatist model of the Asian tigers and the economies of the Pacific Rim (a group of Pacific Ocean countries and islands that constitute more than half of the world's population); others may emulate the social democratic welfare states of western Europe; a few will pursue a more laissez-faire approach; yet others will seek whatever method—either market or planned—that might help them establish a viable place in the international arena. Unfortunately, many are likely to remain destitute for some time. In this fateful drama, considerations of culture and politics are likely to play a more determinative role than any choice of economic instrumentalities.

PROBLEMS WITH SOCIALISM

The socialist experiments of the 20th century were motivated by a genuine interest in improving life for the masses, but the results instead delivered untold suffering in terms of economic depravation and political tyranny. Nonetheless, the egalitarian values that inspired the socialist experiments continue to possess great intellectual and moral appeal. And while socialism has proved less attractive than democratic capitalism, many of the most normatively attractive elements of socialism have been incorporated into democratic systems, as evidenced by public support for spending on social programs.

The chief economic problem of socialism has been the efficient performance of the very task for which its planning apparatus exists—namely, the effective coordination of production and distribution. Modern critics have declared that a planned economy is impossible—i.e., will inevitably become unmanageably chaotic—by virtue of the need for a planning agency to make the millions of dovetailing decisions necessary to produce the gigantic catalog of goods and services of a modern society. Moreover, classical economists would criticize the perverse incentives caused by the absence of private property rights. Precisely such problems became manifest in the late 1980s in the Soviet Union.

The proposed remedy to the problems of socialism involves the use of market arrangements under which managers are free to conduct the affairs of their enterprises according to the dictates of supply and demand (rather than those of a central authority). The difficulty with this solution lies in its political rather than economic requirements, because the acceptance of a market system entrusted with the coordination of the bulk of economic activity requires the tolerance of a sphere of private authority apart from that of public authority. A market mechanism may be compatible with a society of socialist principles, but it requires that the forms of socialist societies as they now exist be radically reorganized. The political difficulties of such a reorganization are twofold. One difficulty arises from the tensions that can be expected to exist between the private interests, and no doubt the public visions, of the managerial echelons and those of the political regime. The creation of a market is tantamount to the creation of a realm within society into which the political arm of government is not allowed to reach fully.

Another political difficulty encountered in the move from socialism to the market is the impact on the working class. The establishment of a market system as the major coordinator of economic activity, including labour services, necessarily introduces the use of unemployment as a disciplining force into a social order. Under socialist planning, government commands were used to allocate employment and thereby did not permit the hiring or firing of workers for strictly economic reasons. The problem with this was inefficient production, underemployment, and misallocations of labour. The introduction of a market mechanism for labour is, however, likely to exacerbate class tensions between workers and management. Some socialist reformers tried to overcome these tensions by increasing worker participation in the management of the enterprises in which they worked, but no great successes have been reported. Finally, socialist governments will tend to encounter problems when they come to rely on market coordinative mechanisms, because economic decentralization and political centralization have inherent incompatibilities.

CONCLUSION

Fundamentally, economics analyzes and describes the consequences of choices made concerning scarce productive resources. Economists study how individuals and societies choose to employ those resources: what goods and services will be produced, how they will be produced, and how they will be distributed among the members of society. The field as it is known today began with the classical school, anchored by such luminaries as Adam Smith, David Ricardo, and John Stuart Mill. Among those who have modified classical economics to reach very different conclusions are Karl Marx and John Maynard Keynes.

The field is customarily divided into microeconomics and macroeconomics. Of major concern to macroeconomists are the rate of economic growth, the inflation rate, and the rate of unemployment. Specialized areas of economic investigation attempt to answer questions on a variety of economic activity; they include agricultural economics, economic development, economic history, environmental economics, industrial organization, international trade, labour economics, money supply and banking, public finance, urban economics, and welfare economics. Specialists in mathematical economics and econometrics provide tools used by all economists. The areas of investigation in economics overlap with many other disciplines, notably history, mathematics, political science, and sociology.

The set of principles and techniques by which a society decides and organizes the ownership and allocation of economic resources is called an economic system. At one extreme, usually called a free-enterprise system, all resources are privately owned. This system, following Adam Smith, is based on the belief that the common good is maximized when all members of society are allowed to pursue their rational self-interest. At the other extreme, usually called a pure-communist system, all resources are publicly owned. This system, following Karl Marx and Vladimir Ilich Lenin, is based on the belief that public ownership of the means of production and government control of every aspect of the economy are necessary to minimize inequalities of wealth and achieve other agreed-upon social objectives.

No nation exemplifies either extreme. As one moves from capitalism through socialism to communism, a greater share of a nation's productive resources is publicly owned and a greater reliance is placed on economic planning.

Economic systems may lose some of the decisive differences that have marked them in the past and come to suggest, instead, a continuum on which elements of both market and planning coexist in different proportions. Societies along such a continuum may continue to designate themselves as either capitalist or socialist, but they are likely to reveal as many similarities as differences in their solutions to economic problems.

GLOSSARY

BOOM AND BUST Alternate periods of high and low levels of economic activity in the business cycle.

COMPARATIVE ADVANTAGE An economic theory, first developed by 19th-century English economist David Ricardo, that attributed the cause and benefits of international trade to the differences among countries in the relative opportunity costs (costs in terms of other goods given up) of producing the same commodities.

CORPORATIST Of or relating to the organization of a society into industrial and professional corporations serving as organs of political representation and exercising control over persons and activities within their jurisdiction.

DEFLATION A contraction in the volume of available money or credit that results in a general decline in prices.

DEPRESSION A period of low general economic activity marked especially by rising levels of unemployment.

EFFICIENCY A measure of the input a system requires to achieve a specified output; a system that uses relatively few resources to achieve its goals is efficient.

ELASTICITY The responsiveness of a dependent economic variable to changes in influencing factors.

EQUILIBRIUM A condition in which opposing economic forces are so balanced that there is no tendency to change in one way or another; a normative position toward which economic forces impel or about which fluctuations occur.

EXTERNALITY A secondary or unintended consequence.

GLASNOST A Soviet policy permitting open discussion of political and social issues and freer dissemination of news and information.

GROSS NATIONAL PRODUCT (GNP) The total market value of the final goods and services produced by a nation's economy during a specific period of time (usually a year), computed before allowance is made for the depreciation or consumption of capital used in the process of production.

INFLATION A continuing rise in the general price level usually attributed to an increase in the volume of money and credit relative to available goods and services.

INPUT-OUTPUT ANALYSIS Economic analysis in which the interdependence of an economy's various productive sectors is observed by viewing the product of each industry both as a commodity demanded for final consumption and as a factor in the production of itself and other goods.

LABOUR The general body of wage earners. In classical economics, labour is one of the three factors of production, along with capital and land. Labour can also be used to describe work performed, including any valuable service rendered by a human agent in the production of wealth, other than accumulating and providing capital.

LAW OF DEMAND The economic statement that the quantity of an economic good purchased will vary inversely with its price.

MONOPOLY Exclusive ownership through legal privilege, command of supply, or concerted action.

MULTIPLIER EFFECT The effect of a relatively small change in one economic factor (such as rate of saving or level of consumer credit) in inducing a disproportionate increase or decrease in another (such as gross national product).

OLIGOPOLY A market situation in which each of a few producers affects but does not control the market. Each producer must consider the effect of a price change on the actions of the other producers.

OPPORTUNITY COST The added cost of using resources (as for production or speculative investment) that is the difference between the actual value resulting from such use and that of an alternative (as another use of the same resources or an investment of equal risk but greater return).

PERESTROIKA Extensive restructuring and reform intended to revitalize the government and economy of the former Soviet Union.

PRODUCTION FUNCTION An equation that expresses the relationship between the quantities of productive factors (such as labour and capital) used and the amount of product obtained. It states the amount of product that can be obtained from every combination of factors, assuming that the most efficient available methods of production are used.

PROLETARIAT The class of industrial workers who lack their own means of production and hence sell their labour to live.

RATIONAL CHOICE A theory that attempts to explain all social phenomena by reference to the activities of rational individuals. It unpacks social facts, institutions, and patterns of rule entirely by analyses of individuals acting in their own self-interest.

RECESSION A downward trend in the business cycle characterized by a decline in production and employment, which in turn causes the incomes and spending of households to decline.

SCARCITY Smallness of quantity or number in proportion to the wants or demands.

TAX INCIDENCE The way in which the burden of a tax is distributed between buyers and producers.

TRANSACTION COST Economic losses that can result from arranging market relationships on a contractual basis.

ECONOMICS

Mark Blaug and Howard R. Vane (eds.), *Who's Who in Economics*, 4th ed. (2003), contains biographical information on 1,500 economists, based on their frequency of citation in economics journals. Mark Blaug, *Great Economists Before Keynes* (1986, reissued 1997), provides thumbnail sketches of the ideas of 200 eminent economists. Douglas Greenwald (ed.), *The McGraw-Hill Encyclopaedia of Economics*, 2nd ed. (1994); and Phillip Anthony O'Hara (ed.), *Encyclopaedia of Political Economy*, 2 vol. (1998, reissued 2001), are two accessible sources of reference addressed to students coming to economics for the first time.

There is the more comprehensive John Eatwell, Murray Milgate, and Peter Newman (eds.), *The New Palgrave: A Dictionary of Economics*, 4 vol. (1987, reissued 2002), but the level of readability and technical difficulty varies greatly from entry to entry. For a more accessible overview, see Roger E. Backhouse, *The Penguin History of Economics* (2002).

Representative introductory textbooks are Paul A. Samuelson and William D. Nordhaus, *Economics*, 18th ed. (2005); Richard G. Lipsey and K. Alec Chrystal, *Economics*, 10th ed. (2004); and William J. Baumol and Alan S. Blinder, *Economics: Principles and Policy*, 9th ed. (2003).

PRICE SYSTEM

The classic work on the history of economic theory, particularly of value theory, is Joseph Schumpeter, *History of Economic Analysis*, ed. by Elizabeth Boody Schumpeter (1954, reissued 1986). Pioneering works on the informational role of the price system are presented in F.A. Hayek, *Individualism and Economic Order* (1948), in particular the essays "The Use of Knowledge in Society" and "Economics and Knowledge." An excellent brief discussion can be found in George J. Stigler, *Essays in the History of Economics* (1965, reprinted 1987), especially essays 5, 6, and 12. Advanced works on modern value theory are J.R. Hicks, *Value and Capital*, 2nd ed. (1950, reissued 1974); and Paul A. Samuelson, *Foundations of Economic Analysis*, enlarged ed. (1983).

Major historical treatises include Adam Smith, *An Inquiry into the Nature and Causes of the Wealth of Nations*, 2 vol. (1776, reissued in 1 vol., 1991); and John Stuart Mill, *Principles of Political Economy*, 2 vol. (1848, reissued in 1 vol., 1994). Selected applied analyses include R.A. Radford, "The Economic Organization of a P.O.W. Camp," *Economica*, 12:189–201 (1945), an account of the evolution of a cigarette-based price system; and Reuben A. Kessel, R.H. Coase, and Merton H. Miller (eds.), *Essays in Applied Price Theory* (1980).

Seminal works in the history of value theory include David Ricardo, *On the Principles of Political Economy and Taxation* (1817, reissued 1981); F.Y. Edgeworth, *Mathematical Psychics* (1881, reprinted 1967); Vilfredo Pareto, *Cours d'économie politique*, 2 vol. (1896–97); J.R. Hicks and R.D.G. Allen, "A Reconsideration of the Theory of Value," *Economica*, New Series, 2 parts, 1:52–76,196–219 (1934); R.G.D. Allen, "Professor Slutsky's Theory of Consumers' Choice," *The Review of Economic Studies*, 3:120–129 (1936); Carl Menger, *Principles of Economics* (1950, reissued 1981; originally published in German, 1871); Léon Walras, *Elements of Pure Economics; or, The Theory of Social Wealth* (1954, reprinted 1984; originally published in French, 1874); W. Stanley Jevons, *The Theory of Political Economy*, 5th ed. (1957); and Alfred Marshall, *Principles of Economics*, 9th ed., 2 vol. (1961), also discussing price.

ECONOMIC SYSTEMS

GENERAL TEXTS

Historical analysis is presented in Robert L. Heilbroner, *The Making of Economic Society*, 11th ed. (2002). An excellent presentation along more functional lines, well-written but requiring some acquaintance with economic theory, is Frederic L. Pryor, *A Guidebook to the Comparative Study of Economic Systems* (1985). Morris Bornstein (ed.), *Comparative Economic Systems: Models and Cases*, 7th ed. (1994), a book of readings, is also recommended.

CAPITALISM

Two broad treatments of capitalism are Adam Smith, *An Inquiry into the Nature and Causes of the Wealth of Nations* (1776); and Karl Marx, *Das Kapital*, vol. 1, trans. by Samuel Moore and Edward Aveling as *Capital: A Critical Analysis of Capitalist Production* (1886); both works are available in many later editions. Robert L. Heilbroner, *The Nature and Logic of Capitalism* (1985), treats the social formation of capitalism. Fernand Braudel, *Civilization and Capitalism, 15th–18th Century*, 3 vol. (1982–84, reissued 1992; originally published in French, 1979), is a wide-ranging overview. Nathan Rosenberg and L.E. Birdzell, Jr., *How the West Grew Rich: The Economic Transformation of the Industrial World* (1986, reissued 1999), discusses the Industrial Revolution and the rise of capitalism. John Kenneth Galbraith, *The New Industrial State*, 4th ed. (1985), is a modern classic. Milton Friedman, *Capitalism and Freedom* (1962, reissued 2002); and Milton Friedman and Rose Friedman, *Free to Choose* (1980, reissued 1990), are perhaps the most accessible treatments of economics and public policy from a market-oriented perspective.

THE SOVIET EXPERIENCE

The classic work on the economic history of the Soviet Union is Alec Nove, *An Economic History of the U.S.S.R., 1917–1991*, 3rd ed. (1992). A political history of the Soviet Union that pays significant attention to the underlying ideology, including political economy, is Martin Malia, *The Soviet Tragedy* (1994, reissued 1996). Ed A. Hewett, *Reforming the Soviet*

Economy: Equality Versus Efficiency (1988), offers thoughtful criticisms and considered appraisals on reforming the Soviet-type economy. Peter J. Boettke, *Why Perestroika Failed: The Politics and Economics of Socialist Transformation* (1993), discusses systemic problems with the Soviet-type system.

SOCIALISM

A history of the debate over the economic feasibility of socialism is available in Don Lavoie, *Rivalry and Central Planning* (1985). A comprehensive reference collection of the main texts in the socialist calculation debate (theoretical comparisons of centrally planned versus free-market economies) can be found in Peter J. Boettke (ed.), *Socialism and the Market: The Socialist Calculation Debate Revisited*, 9 vol. (2000). Other theoretical works include Alec Nove, *The Economics of Feasible Socialism*, 2nd ed. (1991); Branko Horvat, *The Political Economy of Socialism: A Marxist Social Theory* (1982); David L. Prychitko and Jaroslav Vanek (eds.), *Producer Cooperatives and Labor-Managed Systems*, 2 vol. (1996); and János Kornai, *The Socialist System* (1992).

Discussions regarding China, eastern Europe, and the Soviet Union are in Andrei Schleifer and Daniel Treisman, *Without a Map: Political Tactics and Economic Reform in Russia* (2000); Jeffrey Sachs, *Poland's Jump to the Market Economy: The Socialist Calculation Debate Reconsidered* (1993, reissued 1999); and Barry Naughton, *Growing out of the Plan: Chinese Economic Reform, 1978–1993* (1995).

INDEX

A

B

C

D

E

G